The Torch-Bea

A Satirical Comedy in Three Acts

George Kelly

Alpha Editions

This edition published in 2024

ISBN : 9789357957175

Design and Setting By
Alpha Editions
www.alphaedis.com
Email - info@alphaedis.com

Contents

THE TORCH-BEARERS

"The Torch-Bearers," by George Kelly, was presented by Stewart and French for the first time on any stage at the Savoy Theatre, Asbury Park, New Jersey, on the night of Monday, August 14, 1922, with the following cast:

MR. FREDERICK RITTER	MR. ARTHUR SHAW
MR. HUXLEY HOSSEFROSSE	MR. DOUGLAS GARDEN
MR. SPINDLER	MR. EDWARD REESE
MR. RALPH TWILLER	MR. BOOTH HOWARD
TEDDY SPEARING	MR. WILLIAM CASTLE
MR. STAGE MANAGER	MR. J. A. CURTIS
MRS. PAULA RITTER	MISS MARY BOLAND
MRS. J. DURO PAMPINELLI	MISS ALISON SKIPWORTH
MRS. NELLY FELL	MISS HELEN LOWELL
MISS FLORENCE MCCRICKETT	MISS ROSE MARY KING
MRS. CLARA SHEPPARD	MISS DAISY ATHERTON
JENNY	MISS MARY GILDEA

Play staged by the Author

NOTE—

The form of the present manuscript is exactly that in which this play was presented during its run at the Vanderbilt Theatre, New York City, New York.

—The Author.

CAST

MR. FREDERICK RITTER

MR. HUXLEY HOSSEFROSSE

MR. SPINDLER

MR. RALPH TWILLER

TEDDY SPEARING

MR. STAGE MANAGER

MRS. PAULA RITTER (*Ritter's wife*)

MRS. J. DURO PAMPINELLI

MRS. NELLY FELL

MISS FLORENCE MCCRICKETT

MRS. CLARA SHEPPARD

JENNY (*a housemaid at Ritter's*)

SCENE

ACT I— A kind of drawing-room in the home of Frederick Ritter, on an evening in October, about 8 o'clock.

ACT II— Behind the scenes at Horticultural Hall, the following evening at 8:30.

ACT III— The drawing-room at Ritter's, two hours later.

Stage, screen and amateur rights for the production of this play are controlled by the author, George Kelly, 3665 Midvale Avenue, Philadelphia, Pennsylvania. No public readings or performances may be given without his written consent.

PREFACE

I cannot remember if it was one of those torrid and terrible nights of August when the chain-gang of New York's critics was tolled off to the Forty-Eighth Street Theatre for the première of *The Torch-Bearers*. But I do know that the general atmosphere of oppression—physical, mental, professional—was a little denser than usual. In the first twenty-eight days of August, 1922, managements too daring or too resourceless to wait for September had deluged us with a steady stream of inanity, and here was another dousing in prospect. If it wasn't the heat, it was certainly the humidity of theatrical August. Unknown play, new producers, author's name vaguely connected with vaudeville; altogether a production so little esteemed by the booking powers that it had to slip into a few weeks before the Equity Players began their season at this theatre. It could have been a night of Elysian coolness, and still we would have been expecting the worst. It could have been mid-April, and still we should have found an almost ineffable freshness in the breeze of George Kelly's little comedy.

The cold, historical fact is that at about 9:15 o'clock on the evening of August 29th, 1922, five or six hundred average New Yorkers, two or three hundred friends of the management, and about fifty sophisticated first-nighters were in grave danger of rolling off their seats in hysteria because of *The Torch-Bearers*.

The intermissions were filled with three questions which more or less concern the reader of the published play. Who was George Kelly? Where did he get the comedy? How would it go?

On August 29th, 1922, George Kelly was a perfectly good Philadelphian in his late twenties who was much better known to vaudeville than to fame. He had written, directed, and played in about a dozen one-act comedies and dramas on Keith and Orpheum time. He had begun by quitting his family's private tutor to try acting in a playlet by the late Paul Armstrong. Then—with no more preparation, apparently—he had begun to write his own vehicles. A certain drama in France absorbed his attentions for a while. After that more "sketches"—as the vaudeville powers call any effort above vocal or bodily acrobatics—and suddenly a play.

The origin of *The Torch-Bearers* was simple enough. Kelly wrote the kind of tight, effective short plays that amateur actors and little theatre directors are always looking for. He had a perfectly good Philadelphia family behind him. And so he was being invited to lunch every now and then by the Pampinellis of the cities in which he played. To hear them was enough. They had to live a wider life.

The Torch-Bearers passed a prosperous term on Broadway, and I think it will go far in the little theatres which it satirizes. But upon the opening night I remember much dubious debate about its chances. We had laughed ourselves almost literally sick, and at the end of the second intermission we had not yet seen the rather prosy last act. Yet—conscious of our personal superiority— we wondered.... Brander Matthews and Aristotle would scoff at it, George M. Cohan and Professor Baker would scowl. *The Torch-Bearers* broke all the rules, and it had no plot. Obviously, by all the rules, it ought to fail.

There may be a good many reasons why it didn't, and some may lead you far into aesthetic explorations of the present breakdown of dramatic form all over the world. But the reader will find more cogent reasons in the pages that follow this introduction. Personally, I should put it down to the fact that the character-study of the first act and the hokum of the second are irresistible. We have all met our Pampinellis, and we have all seen the lady prompter take a curtain call, or had our mustache fall off in the big scene. We can never resist some characterization on the stage, and as for such hokum as this record of all the mishaps of the amateur actor, ill luck is the heart of broad comedy and when ill luck comes where it is most painful—in personal display—Cassandra herself must smile.

There were other things to make the death-watch wonder whether *The Torch Bearers* could live. It was satire. Satire is not ordinarily a popular commodity in the theatre. It defeats sympathy, and sympathy is necessary to emotion, and emotion to theatrical success.

Satire has had its great moments, however, in the history of the drama. Aristophanes made merry over the fashions, foibles, and philosophies of Athens. Satire was Molière's stock in trade. Shaw has done very well by poking a finger at society. Every nation has at least one outstanding theatrical satire to its credit. But for the war, the wise of Paris might still be laughing at the French Academy because of de Flers and de Caillavet's *L'Habit Vert*. England has *The School for Scandal*, as Ireland has *The Playboy* and *John Bull's Other Island*. Germany, though a little heavy in the theatre, can still point to Schnitzler's *Literature*.

Just at the moment America is beginning to display a surprising fondness for theatrical satire. Beginning is hardly the word, perhaps, for the first American drama, *The Contrast*, lampooned society with a large "S"; *Fashion*, our first play by a woman, spoke out smartly against the smart world, and from *Our American Cousin* down to date, so many of our playwrights have spoofed the alien and the aristocratic for the benefit of the homespun, that it is only by a hair that I can risk the statement that it is a "surprising fondness" which we now display for satire. America has always enjoyed its irreverent moments in the theatre, but it has seldom gone in for whole plays devoted to almost nothing but lampooning.

In the last three seasons, however, the distinctly satirical play has climbed noticeably in favour. In 1919-20 there was nothing of the kind to be seen on Broadway. In 1920-21 came Porter Emerson Browne's Mexican melodrama, *The Bad Man*, with most of its success due to sly digs at both sides of the international line, and George M. Cohan's joke at the expense of audiences as well as playwrights, *The Tavern*. Last season, playgoers good-humoredly made a satire out of the deadly serious absurdities of the British melodrama, *Bulldog Drummond*; the *Chauve-Souris* twitted Russian drama a little—in Russian; and the firm of Kaufman and Connelly began in *Dulcy* and *To the Ladies!* to vend biting wit at the expense of scenario writers and advertisers, efficiency experts and after-dinner speakers.

This season a perfect flood of satire broke upon us, most of it very good indeed, and some of it destined to be successful with a large public. Besides *The Torch-Bearers*, there have been *R. U. R.*, grim sarcasm upon labour and capital, and a new bill of the *Chauve-Souris*, the Kaufman-Connelly version of Henry Leon Wilson's *Merton of the Movies*, *Six Characters in Search of an Author*, from the Italian, and *The World We Live In*, the insect comedy from the Czecho-Slovak.

The future of *The Torch-Bearers*, now that its Broadway career is over, brings us up against the little theatre movement. I am very much in favor of that odd and amazing phenomenon. I believe a great deal of the promise of the American stage outside New York and a surprising amount of its present accomplishment in that metropolis, is due to the uncontrollable desire of people not so very unlike Mrs. Pampinelli to produce plays. Kelly's satire touches the lower fringes of what Mrs. P. calls "the movement," but it might be directed at Maurice Browne, Sam Hume, and Irving Pichel and the little theatre would still go on, and *The Torch-Bearers* would become—as I am sure it will—one of the most popular pieces in the repertory of the amateur actor. Many a Mrs. Pampinelli, safe in the sense of her own self-importance, will do for *The Torch-Bearers* all that Mrs. P. did—which is, as Kelly observes, to "tell the players where to go on the stage, so they won't be running into each other."

But there is art in this play—not mere observation—and I am afraid none of the Pampinellis who are to be concerned with its future will ever quite equal the person that the author and Alison Skipworth, the actress, created between them. I do not look for any moment so extraordinary as when Mrs. Pampinelli, discussing the fatalities invariably connected with these amateur performances, reaches her peroration: "We are not dismayed; we have the lessons of history to fortify us: for whenever the torch of essential culture has been raised, (*she raises the lead-pencil as though it were a torch*) there has unfailingly been the concomitant exactment of a human life." For one cannot expect to find a cuckoo-clock always present with its sapient comment at such a moment.

The reader will find the cuckoo-clock, the satire, and the hokum for himself. He will also detect, I think, a strain of divine and devilish madness in Kelly which promises something of genius for the American drama. The reader may note, too, in Kelly's script the kind of practical qualification for the theatre of which Mr. Ritter speaks feelingly on page 56. This qualification has produced extraordinarily effective humor and something else. This is a sense for stage management. It makes Kelly a rare and precious figure in our theatre, and gives you a script to read—or to produce—that is liberally supplied with every bit of business and direction necessary for putting on the play—either in the Cohoes Little Theatre or your own imagination.

KENNETH MACGOWAN.

Pelham Manor, N. Y., February 25, 1923.

NOTE: The drawing-room at Ritter's, in which the first and last acts are laid, is a comfortable-looking room, suggestive of good circumstance. Toward the back there is a fancy wooden partition separating the hallway from the room proper. This partition begins rather high up on the side walls and curves deeply down to two ornamental columns, five feet high and set about five feet apart, forming the entrance from the hallway to the room. Straight out through this entrance, and paralleling the partition, is the staircase, running up to the left and through an arched doorway. The foot of the staircase is just to the right of the center-door; and then the hallway continues on out to the front door. On the left, there is a passageway between the staircase and the partition, running through an arched doorway to the body of the house. In the room proper, breaking the angle of the right wall and the partition, is a door, opening out, and below this door, a casement-window. On the left, breaking the angle of the left wall and the partition, is the mantelpiece, and below it a door, opening out. Just inside the partition, on either side of the center-door, is a built-in seat.

The entire room and hallway is done in a scheme of silver and the lighter shades of green. All the woodwork and furniture, including the piano and mantelpiece, is finished in silver-green, and the walls and ceiling are in blended tones of orchid, gray and green, decorated with tapestried panel-effects. The carpet is gray-green, and the vases and clock on the mantelpiece, as well as the little cuckoo-clock over the door at the left, are green. The drapes on the casement-window and the doorways, at the head of the stairs and in the left hallway, are in rose-colored brocaded satin; and the pads on the partition-seats are covered with the same material. The piano-throw is a garishly subdued blend of old-rose, Nile green and canary-colored silk.

Right out between the little wooden columns of the center-door, set flat against the staircase, is a small console-table, holding a most beautiful rose-colored vase filled with wisteria; and on the piano there is a similar vase filled with white and yellow blossoms. On either side of the console-table there is a tall torchiere with a rose-colored shade; and the shades on the wall-lights, and the one on the lovely rose-colored vase-lamp on the table down at the right below the casement-window, are all rose-colored.

There's a brilliant array of cushions about the room, all shapes and sizes, and every color of the rainbow,—and many books and magazines. The piano, up at the right, is littered with music, cigarettes, in a fancy container, flowers and candy—in a pretty box made of pink satin.

The two arm-chairs in the room, one just to the left of the table below the window, and the other at the left side of the table over at the left, are over-stuffed in green-and-silver brocade.

There is a small table below the piano, with a light little chair beside it, the left side, and there is a similar chair over at the extreme left, below the door.

The keyboard of the piano parallels the right wall, with enough room, of course, between the piano-stool and wall to permit of easy use of the door. There must also be room enough above the piano for a passageway between it and the partition-seat.

The rights and lefts employed in the foregoing descriptions are, of course, the player's rights and lefts.

ACT ONE.

After a slight pause, a door out at the right is heard to close, and immediately Mr. Ritter comes along the hallway beyond the partition and into the room. He is a brisk, rather stocky type of man, in his early forties, wearing a brown suit and overcoat, a derby hat, and carrying a suit-case. He sets the suit-case down on the partition-seat at the right, and, with a glance around the room, at the unusual arrangement of the furniture, starts out into the hallway again, removing his gloves and overcoat. He glances along the hallway to the left and up the stairs as he goes. Jenny comes along the hallway from the left carrying a small, light chair. As she is about to come into the drawing-room proper from the hallway, she becomes conscious of Mr. Ritter out at the hall-rack at the right. She stops and peers in that direction. She is a pleasant little English person, plump and trim, dressed in the regulation parlor-maid's black and white.

JENNY. Is that you, Mr. Ritter?

RITTER. That's who it is, Jenny! How are you?

JENNY. [*Bringing the little chair forward and placing it above the little table at the left*] Pretty well, thanks, Mr. Ritter, how are *you*?

RITTER. [*Coming along the hallway from the right*] I'm whatever you are, Jenny. [*Jenny gives a faint little laugh and proceeds with her arrangements, and Ritter picks up several telegrams from the stand in the hallway, just to the left of the center entrance.*]

JENNY. Ain't you back a bit soon?

RITTER. [*Coming forward to the small table at the right, below the piano*] Yes, I thought I'd have to go down to Cincinnati for a week or two, but I didn't.

JENNY. Mrs. Ritter ain't expectin' you, is she?

RITTER. [*Glancing thru the telegrams*] No, she isn't, Jenny.

JENNY. I thought I didn't remember hearin' her sayin' nothin'.

RITTER. Where is she?

JENNY. [*Starting for the hallway*] She's upstairs, sir, I'll call her.

RITTER. [*With a glance at the furniture*] What are you doing around here, Jenny, housecleaning?

JENNY. [*Turning and coming back*] No, sir, there's a rehearsal here tonight. [*Ritter stops reading and looks at her quizzically for a second.*]

RITTER. What kind of a rehearsal?

JENNY. Why, a rehearsal for a show that Mrs. Ritter's takin' part in tomorrow night. They done it at the Civic Club the week after you went away, and they liked it so well they're doin' it again tomorrow night.

- 9 -

RITTER. *Who* liked it?

JENNY. Sir?

RITTER. I say, who liked it so well that they're doing it again?

JENNY. Why, everybody seemed to like it, Mr. Ritter, from what the papers said.

RITTER. What kind of a show is it?

JENNY. Why, I think it's a tragedy, from what I gather.

RITTER. Did you see it, Jenny?

JENNY. No, sir, *I* didn't get to see it, I'm sorry to say; but I heard everybody connected with it sayin' it was a *great success.* [*Ritter resumes his telegrams, then looks at Jenny suddenly.*]

RITTER. How did Mrs. Ritter get into it?

JENNY. Why, I think somebody died, Mr. Ritter, if I'm not mistaken.

RITTER. [*Shaking his head conclusively, and resuming his telegram*] I assumed it was an extremity of *some* kind.

MRS. R. [*At the top of the stairs at the back*] Fred Ritter! don't tell me that's you down there! [*Jenny turns quickly and goes to the foot of the stairs.*]

RITTER. No, I'm still out in Chicago!

MRS. R. Is it, Jenny?

JENNY. Yes, mam, I was just comin' to tell you.

MRS. R. [*Starting down the stairs*] I *thought* I heard his voice! [*Jenny laughs.*] I've been standing up here for the last *five* minutes saying to myself, "Who can that *be* that has a voice so much like Fred's!" [*Coming into the room from the hallway*] Why, Fred, darling, what are you doing here! [*He has moved up towards the center-door.*]

RITTER. [*Laughing a little*] How is the old kid! [*Kisses her*]

MRS. R. I thought you wouldn't be back till the first! [*Jenny passes along the hallway to the left.*]

RITTER. Why, that Cincinnati thing's been postponed till after Thanksgiving.

MRS. R. [*Turning away from him and stepping out into the hallway again*] Well, why didn't you wire or something?

RITTER. I was afraid of giving you a shock.

MRS. R. Oh, Jenny!

RITTER. You're such a frail little flower.

MRS. R. [*Turning back to him*] Now stop, Fred! I've really lost a lot since you went away.

RITTER. How do you know? [*Jenny comes along the hallway from the left.*]

MRS. R. Why, my dear, I can tell by my clothes. [*She turns to Jenny.*] Jenny, will you get me a glass of water, please.

JENNY. [*Starting out*] Yes, mam.

RITTER. You're not going to faint, are you?

MRS. R. [*Turning back to him again with a flip of her hand at him*] No, I'm not.

RITTER. [*Slipping his arm around her waist and coming forward*] Any mail here for me?

MRS. R. Not a single thing, Fred; I sent everything right on to Chicago as soon as it came: there must be several letters there for you now.

RITTER. [*Disengaging himself and taking her hands and looking at her*] I'll get them all right. How have you been treating yourself while I've been away?

MRS. R. All right; only I'm glad to see you back.

RITTER. Kiss me.

MRS. R. The house seemed awfully lonesome.

RITTER. Kiss me. [*She kisses him.*]

MRS. R. [*Passing above him to the piano at the right*] Crazy thing. [*He moves over to the little table at the left, rummaging in his pocket for a cigar, and Mrs. Ritter commences to rummage in a sewing-basket on the piano. This basket is Mrs. Ritter at a glance, all green and yellow satin, fraught with meaningless bows and weird looking knots. She undoubtedly made it herself, and it must have taken her months. But she's a practical woman; at least she thinks she is; and the sewing-basket helps in a way to sustain the conviction. Poor Paula! As one looks at her and listens to her he appreciates the fortune of the circumstance that there is some sane and capable person between her and the world; and as he more closely observes the sewing-basket, he rejoices in the blessing of the sane and capable person's ability to spare her the necessity of having to make her own clothes. Although, as a matter of fact, she would look lovely in anything; for Paula is pretty—charmingly so. And her hair is marvelous. So gold—and satiny. She is wearing a dress now of lime-green silk with a standing collar edged with black fur, and gold-colored slippers.*] Did you have anything to eat, Fred?

RITTER. Yes, I ate on the train. What's this Jenny was saying? Something about a show you're in?

MRS. R. Oh,—[*Looking at him*] did she tell you?

RITTER. I wondered what had happened to the furniture when I came in.

MRS. R. [*Coming around and forward towards the little table below the piano*] Yes, there's a rehearsal here tonight. We have it every Tuesday and Thursday. Of course, it's just to run over the lines, because we've done it already at the Civic Club on the fourteenth. And, my dear, it was perfectly marvelous.

RITTER. What kind of a show is it?

MRS. R. [*Standing back of the table*] Oh, it's just a one-act play,—in one act, you know. And it was really *quite* wonderful. [*She gives an inane laugh.*] I had no idea. [*She touches her hair and turns towards the back of the room again.*]

RITTER. How did *you* happen to get into it? [*Jenny comes along the hallway from the left carrying a glass of water on a small tray.*]

MRS. R. [*Turning to him*] Well now, wait till I tell you—[*She sees Jenny.*] Oh, thanks, Jenny. [*Jenny starts out again.*] Jenny, will you go to the top of the stairs and see if I left the lights burning in my room.

JENNY. [*Turning and starting towards the foot of the stairs in the right hallway; and setting the tray on the little stand as she goes*] Yes, mam.

MRS. RITTER. [*Coming forward holding the glass of water*] I think I did. [*She sips.*]

JENNY. [*As she crosses the center-door*] Do you want that suit-case taken up, Mr. Ritter? [*Mrs. Ritter turns round to the right and watches Jenny.*]

RITTER. Yes, you can take it up if you will, Jenny, thanks. [*Jenny lifts the suit-case from the partition-seat and goes out and up the stairs.*]

MRS. RITTER. [*Turning to Ritter*] You know, I wrote you about poor Jimmy Sheppard—

RITTER. Yes, what was that, had he been sick?

MRS. RITTER. Why, not a day, my dear! that's the reason it was all so dreadful. Of course, he'd always had more or less of a weak heart; but nothing to threaten anything of that kind. And just three days before the performance, mind you:—couldn't happen any other time. And *poor* Mrs. Sheppard playing one of the *leading* parts. [*She turns to her left and goes up to the center-door, where she looks out toward the right hallway expectantly.*]

RITTER. [*Casually depositing the band from his cigar on the tray at his left*] Did he *know* she was to play one of the leading parts?

MRS. RITTER. [*Turning at the center-door and looking at him*] Who,—Mr. Sheppard?

RITTER. Yes.

MRS. RITTER. [*Coming forward again*] Why, of course he did—She'd just finished telling him when he fell over. [*Ritter appears to be unduly occupied with his cigar, and Mrs. Ritter takes advantage of the circumstance to refresh herself with another sip from the glass.*] My dear, poor Clara Sheppard is a *wreck*—You want to write her a note, Fred, when you get time. And he never spoke—not a solitary word. But, she says—just as he was dying,—he gave her the funniest look. Oh, she says—if she lives to be a thousand, she'll *never* forget the way he looked at her. [*She goes up to the center-door and sets the glass down on the tray.*]

RITTER. [*Still busy with his cigar*] Had he ever seen her act?

MRS. RITTER. [*Turning to him, thoughtfully*] I don't know,—whether he ever had or not. [*Jenny comes down the stairs.*] Oh, yes he had, too! for I saw him myself at the Century Drawing Rooms last Easter Monday night, and she was in that play there that night, you remember. [*She moves to the piano and starts looking for something in the sewing-basket; he moves to the mantelpiece, up at the left, apparently looking for a match.*]

RITTER. No, I wasn't there.

MRS. R. Oh, weren't you! I thought you were.

RITTER. No. [*He feels in his pockets.*]

MRS. R. There are matches there on that little table there, Fred. [*She indicates the table below the mantelpiece.*]

RITTER. [*Discovering some in his pocket*] I have some here. [*He moves to the arm-chair at the left of table and sits down.*]

MRS. R. [*As Jenny passes along the hallway towards the left*] Oh, Jenny!

JENNY. Yes, mam?

MRS. R. Jenny, will you ask Mrs. Brock if she'll make some of that drink that she made the last time?

JENNY. I think she 'as made it already, Mrs. Ritter.

MRS. R. Well, will you see, Jenny, please?

JENNY. [*Starting away*] Yes, mam.

MRS. R. [*To Ritter*] The folks liked it so much the last time. [*She picks up her sewing-basket.*]

JENNY. All right, Mrs. Ritter. [*She disappears at the left.*]

MRS. R. [*Stepping out into the hallway*] Oh, and, Jenny!

JENNY. [*Out at the left*] Yes, mam?

MRS. R. Tell her to put a little of that *gin* in it, the way she did before.

JENNY. All right, mam.

MRS. R. Tell her she'll find some gin in the little buffet in the big dining-room.

RITTER. She probably knows where it is.

MRS. R. [*Coming forward carrying her sewing-basket*] Well, anyway, that's how I happened to get into it. [*She sits on the chair at the left of the small table below the piano.*] Mrs. Pampinelli called me up the first thing in the morning, and she said—

RITTER. Is she in it, too?

MRS. R. [*Looking up from the arrangement of a couple of strips of lace which she has taken from the sewing-basket*] Who? Mrs. Pampinelli?

RITTER. Yes.

MRS. R. No, she doesn't take any part; she's just in charge of everything.

RITTER. That suits her better.

MRS. R. Kind of directress, I suppose you'd call her. [*He has some difficulty keeping his face straight.*] Tells us where to go, you know, on the stage,—so we won't be running into each other. [*Ritter laughs.*] Really, Fred, you have no idea how easy it is to run into somebody on the stage. You've got to know where you're going every time you move. [*He laughs louder.*] Why, what are you laughing at?

RITTER. I was just thinking of a few of the things I've heard Mrs. Pampinelli called.

MRS. R. [*Looking over at him reproachfully*] Oh—now, that isn't a bit nice of you, Fred Ritter. I know you don't like her.

RITTER. I like her all right.

MRS. R. No, you do not, now, Fred,—so *don't* say you do.

RITTER. I think she's marvelous.

MRS. R. Well, she's tremendously clever at this stage business, I don't care what you say. You just ought to hear her talk about it sometime. Now, the last rehearsal we had,—over at her house,—she spoke on "Technique in Acting as Distinguished from Method;" and you've no idea how interesting it was. [*Ritter glances over at her as he deposits some ashes from his cigar on the little table-tray.*]

- 14 -

RITTER. You say you've given this show before?

MRS. R. Oh yes! We gave it on the fourteenth at the Civic Club. And, my dear, that audience just loved it. And you'd be surprised too, for it's a terrifically serious thing. In fact, in a way, it's too serious—for the general public—that's the reason several of the people who saw it suggested that, if we give it again, we should give a dance right after it. [*She looks closely at her needle and Ritter looks discreetly at the end of his cigar.*] But, as Mrs. Pampinelli says, it's an absolute impossibility to give a dance at either the Civic Club or the Century Drawing Rooms, so that's how we're giving it this time down at Hutchy Kutchy. [*Ritter looks over at her with a quizzical squint.*]

RITTER. Where?

MRS. R. [*Looking over at him*] Horticultural Hall—there at Broad and Spruce, you know.

RITTER. Yes, I know;—what did *you* call it?

MRS. R. Hutchy Kutchy. [*She laughs inanely.*] Mrs. Pampinelli always calls it that,—I suppose I've gotten into the habit too, from hearing her. [*She gives another little laugh, then finishes with an amused sigh.*]

RITTER. What's the show for, a charity of some kind?

MRS. RITTER. [*Turning to him suddenly, and with a shade of practicality*] It's for the Seamen's Institute. Kind of a refuge for them, you know, while they're in port; so the sailors won't be wandering around the streets getting into bad company. [*Ritter disposes of more ashes, with an unusual precision, and Mrs. Ritter resumes her sewing. Then, suddenly, she glances toward the casement-window at the right.*] It was Mrs. Pampinelli's idea, [*She gathers her things into the sewing-basket and gets up, swinging round to her left and talking as she goes.*] so of course she *didn't* want anything to happen. [*She sets the sewing-basket down on the piano, and, with another glance thru the window at the right, crosses to the little table at the left where Ritter is sitting.*] So she called me up the first thing in the morning, and she said, "Paula darling, *have* you heard the news?" So, of course, I said "No;" because up to that time I *hadn't*, and, naturally, I *wasn't* going to say that I had.

RITTER. Certainly *not.*

MRS. R. "Well," she said, "*poor* Jimmy Sheppard has *just* passed on." Well, luckily, I was sitting down at the time, or I *positively* think I should have passed on myself.

RITTER. [*Raising his hand from the table as though distressed by the extremity of her remarks*] Don't say such things.

MRS. R. [*Mistaking his attitude*] No, really, Fred, you've no idea the *feeling* that came over me when she said that. "Well," I said, "Betty, what on earth are we going to do!" Because the tickets were all sold, you know. "Well," she said, "Paula,—the only thing *I* see to do, is to have *you* step right into Clara Sheppard's role." "Me!" I said. "Yes," she said; "you are the only person in *my* opinion who is qualified to play the part." "But, my dear," I said, "I've never stepped on a stage in my *life!*" "That is absolutely inconsequential," she said, "it is entirely a matter of dramatic instinct. And," she said, [*She simpers a bit here and moves around from the right of the little table where she has been standing to the back of her husband's chair, at the left of the table.*] "*you* have *that*—to a far greater degree than you've *any* idea of." [*He makes a sound of dry amusement.*] No, really, Fred, everyone was saying it was a positive tragedy that you couldn't have been there to see me—I never forgot myself once. [*She rests her hand on his left shoulder, and he reaches up and takes her hand.*]

RITTER. What are you going to do now, become an actress?

MRS. R. No, but it surprised me so, the way everybody enthused; because I didn't think I'd done anything so extraordinary—I just walked onto the stage, and said what I'd been told to say, and walked off again. [*She emphasizes this last phrase by an indefinite gesture of nonchalance in the direction of the door at her left.*] And yet everybody seemed to think it was wonderful. Why, Nelly Fell said she'd never seen even a *professional actress* so absolutely unconscious. [*He makes a sound of amusement.*] Really, Fred, you ought to have heard them. Why, they said if they didn't know, they never in the *world* would have believed that it was my first offense.

RITTER. You mustn't believe everything these women tell you; they'll tell you anything to get their names in the paper.

MRS. R. Well, it wasn't only they that said it;—people that I didn't even *know* said it. Why, Mrs. Pampinelli had a letter from a woman away out at Glenside that happened to see the performance, and she said that, at times, my repose was *positively* uncanny. And the papers simply raved; especially "The Evening Breeze." I have it upstairs, I must show it to you. It said that it didn't understand *how* I had escaped the public eye so long. [*She glances at the cuckoo-clock over the door at the left, and, in doing so, notices a book that has been left lying on the chair below the door: she steps over and picks it up.*] I was awfully sorry you couldn't have been there, Fred. I was going to write you about it when Mrs. Pampinelli first spoke to me about going on, but there was so little time, you see. And then, I didn't think you'd mind;—especially on account of its being for charity. [*He is very carefully putting ashes on the little tray. She stands holding the book, looking at him. And there is a slight pause.*] You *don't* mind my going on, do you, Fred?

RITTER. [*Rather slowly*] No,—I don't mind, if you're able to get away with it.

MRS. R. [*Trailing across back of his chair*] I didn't think you would.

RITTER. [*Raising his hand from the table quietly*] But a—[*She comes to a stop and regards him over her left shoulder.*] I don't want any of these women exploiting you for their own vanity. [*She doesn't quite encompass his meaning, and stands looking at him for a second. Then she abstractedly lays the book down on the table beside him. There is a very definite ring at the front door-bell.*] I guess that's some of the people. [*She starts towards the hallway.*]

RITTER. [*Preparing to rise*] Where do you do this thing, here?

MRS. R. [*Turning to him and indicating the general arrangement*] Yes—just the way we have it fixed.

RITTER. [*Rising briskly and crossing to the table below the piano at the right, while Mrs. R. continues to the center-door and stands looking toward the front door. Jenny appears in the left hallway.*] I think I'll beat it upstairs.

MRS. R. [*Turning to Jenny*] I guess that's some of the people, Jenny. [*She comes forward towards Ritter again.*]

JENNY. Yes, mam. [*She passes back of Mrs. Ritter and along out into the right hallway to answer the door.*]

MRS. R. Won't you wait and see the rehearsal, Fred? [*He is gathering up the telegrams from the table, where he left them earlier.*]

RITTER. [*Turning and going up towards the center-door, thrusting the telegrams into his inside pocket*] No, I think I'd rather wait and see the show. [*He passes her, to her left.*]

MRS. R. [*Turning and trailing up towards the center-door after him*] It's really *very* interesting.

MRS. PAMPINELLI. [*Out at the front door*] You see how considerate I am of you, Jenny, letting myself in? [*Mr. and Mrs. Ritter stop in the center-door and look toward the front door.*]

JENNY. [*At the front door*] Oh, that's all right, Mrs. Pampinelli.

MRS. R. [*Turning quickly to Ritter at her left*] You can't go up now, Fred, she'll see you.

MRS. PAMPINELLI and RITTER, together.

> MRS. P. Well, I daresay you'll have to open this door quite often enough tonight without my troubling you.
>
> RITTER. [*Coming back into the room with a slight gesture of annoyance*] I don't want to have to listen to her gab. [*He goes over to the mantelpiece at the left and takes up his position there, while*

Mrs. Ritter, with a movement to him to be silent, drifts down beside the piano at the right.]

MRS. PAMPINELLI. [*Coming into view from the right hallway*] Well, I suppose I'm still the shining example of punctuality. [*She sweeps thru the center-door, carrying a large black-bear muff, a fan of black ostrich-plumes, and a note-book and pencil.*] How do you do, Mr. Ritter,—[*She goes towards Mrs. Ritter.*]

RITTER. [*Nodding*] How do you do.

MRS. PAMPINELLI. I'm glad to see you.

MRS. RITTER. [*Moving towards Mrs. P.*] Hello, Betty.

MRS. PAMPINELLI. Hello, Paula child,—[*Kisses her*] how are you, dear? [*Mr. Spindler hurries in from the right hallway, carrying several books. Mrs. P. steps to the table below the piano.*] Will you give those things to Mrs. Ritter, Mr. Spindler, she'll set them down somewhere. [*She sets her own encumbrances down on the table, and Mrs. Ritter passes back of her to Spindler.*]

SPINDLER. [*Standing in the middle of the room, toward the back*] Certainly, certainly.

MRS. RITTER. Good evening, Mr. Spindler.

SPINDLER. Good evening, good evening. [*Jenny comes in from the right hallway, takes the tray and glass from the hall table, and goes out the left hallway.*]

MRS. RITTER. I'll just take these.

SPINDLER. [*Giving her the books and a manuscript*] If you please.

MRS. PAMPINELLI. [*Crossing directly to Ritter*] Florence McCrickett told me you were back; she saw you getting into a taxicab at the station. [*Giving him her hand*] I'm glad to see you.

RITTER. I just got in.

MRS. PAMPINELLI. And I suppose you've already heard about the great event?

RITTER. Yes, she's just been telling me. [*They laugh together.*]

MRS. PAMPINELLI. Well, my dear, you may count that day lost that you missed it. [*She half turns to Mrs. Ritter, who is engaged in conversation with Spindler.*] Mayn't he, Paula? [*But Paula hasn't heard what she's been saying, so she just looks at her and gives an inane little laugh. Mrs. Pampinelli continues to Ritter.*] Although you'll have an opportunity tomorrow night; unless you're going to run away again before that.

RITTER. No, I'll be here now till after Thanksgiving. [*Mrs. Ritter leaves Spindler and goes over to a small table at the extreme right, below the casement-window, where she sets the books and manuscript down.*]

MRS. PAMPINELLI. [*Turning from Ritter and crossing back again to the table at the right below the piano*] Wonderful! Did you hear that, Paula?

MRS. R. What is it, dear?

MRS. PAMPINELLI. Mr. Ritter says he will be here for the performance tomorrow night.

MRS. R. Yes.

MRS. PAMPINELLI. [*Unfastening her fur neckpiece*] So you will have an opportunity after all of revealing to him what gems of talent the unfathomed caves of matrimony bear. [*They both laugh.*]

MRS. R. [*Picking up Mrs. Pampinelli's muff from the table and taking the neckpiece*] I'll just take these, Betty.

MRS. PAMPINELLI. [*Settling her beads*] Anywhere at all, dear. [*Mrs. R. starts to the right.*] Oh, and by the way, Paula—[*Mrs. Ritter stops and turns to her.*]

MRS. R. Yes?

MRS. PAMPINELLI. [*Indicating the books on the table below the window*] There's a remarkable article in one of those books I brought, on a—gesture.

MRS. R. [*Looking at the books*] Yes?

MRS. PAMPINELLI. The little gray book I think it is, if I'm not mistaken. [*She turns to her left and acknowledges Mr. Spindler with a touch of state.*] Mr. Spindler— [*He returns a smiling and very snappy little bow.*] brought it to my attention,—[*She turns back again to Paula, who has gone up at the right of the piano and is putting the furs on the partition-seat, while Spindler, becoming suddenly conscious that Ritter is looking at him, stiffens abruptly, glances at Ritter, and turns back again to Mrs. Pampinelli.*] and it really is remarkable. So many of my own ideas—things that I have been advocating for years. I brought it especially for *you*, Paula,—so you must read it when you have time. [*She picks up her lead-pencil from the little table and, tapping it against her right temple, thinks profoundly.*] What is that wonderful line of Emerson's that I'm so fond of—something about our unexpressed thoughts coming back to accuse us—[*Turning to Spindler*] You know all those things, Mr. Spindler.

SPINDLER. [*Pedantically*] Coming back to us "with an alienated majesty."

MRS. PAMPINELLI. That is the one I mean. [*She turns back again to Paula, who has, by this time, come forward again at the right of the piano, while Mr. Spindler, again becoming conscious that Ritter is looking at him, gives him another glance, this time with* a shade of resentment in it, and, coughing briefly, as an emphasis of his dignity, which Ritter's general attitude somehow suggests is not being sufficiently esteemed, turns back to Mrs. Pampinelli.] Well, that is exactly what occurred to me when I read that article—My own thoughts returning to me from an alienated majesty. [She finishes her version of the quotation to Spindler and Mr. Ritter.] Oh, by the way,— [She gives a little mirthless laugh.] I'm afraid I've neglected to introduce Mr. Spindler [Indicating Ritter with a very casual gesture of her left hand, and picking up her lead-pencil from the little table] This is Mrs. Ritter's husband, Mr. Spindler. [Spindler strides towards Ritter and extends his hand with that vigor which usually characterizes the greetings of unimportant persons.]

SPINDLER. Glad!

RITTER. [Tonelessly] How are you?

MRS. PAMPINELLI. [Addressing Ritter directly] Mr. Spindler is a young man who has made quite an exhaustive study of the Little Theatre Movement throughout the country; [Spindler moves back towards his former position, and Paula, over at the right, takes a piece of fudge from a box on the little table below the casement-window.] and is working very hard to bring about something of the same kind here. [Ritter inclines his head, and Spindler listens to Mrs. Pampinelli, wreathed in smiles.] And is going to succeed, too, aren't you, Mr. Spindler?

SPINDLER. [With a kind of pert assurance] Never fell down on a big job yet. [He gives a self-conscious little laugh and glances at Ritter, under whose coldly-appraising eye the laugh freezes instantly into a short, hollow cough. Then he turns away.]

MRS. PAMPINELLI. I'm sure he has all the qualifications.

SPINDLER. [With a wooden smile, and saluting] Thank you, thank you.

MRS. PAMPINELLI. Hasn't he, Paula?

MRS. RITTER. [Nibbling at the fudge] Yes indeed, Mr. Spindler's quite indispensable. [Spindler gives her a pert little nod, by way of acknowledgment.]

MRS. PAMPINELLI. [To Mrs. Ritter] I think that's what I shall have to call him hereafter,—[Turning to Spindler] the indispensable Mr. Spindler. [They all laugh,—a trifle more than the brilliancy of the remark should reasonably occasion, and Mr. Spindler accounts it even worthy a salute.]

SPINDLER. Bouquets were falling [Here the front door-bell gives two sharp little staccato rings.] thick and fast. [He starts towards the center-door.]

MRS. PAMPINELLI. Well, it's true—

SPINDLER. [Speaking directly to Mrs. Ritter] I'll answer it. [He hurries out into the right hallway.]

MRS. P. and MRS. R., speaking together.

MRS. P. I know I don't know what on earth I should do without him.

MRS. R. [*Addressing Spindler as he hurries out the hallway*] All right, if you will, Mr. Spindler.

SPINDLER. [*Calling back*] Sure!

MRS. PAMPINELLI. He is one of those rare persons who never forsakes one in the hour of quotation. [*She turns to Mrs. Ritter, who is chewing fudge at her right.*] What are you eating, Paula?

MRS. RITTER. A bit of fudge. Would you like some, Betty?

MRS. PAMPINELLI. [*Very definitely*] No, thank you, dear.

MRS. RITTER. [*Indicating the table below the casement-window*] There's some here.

MRS. PAMPINELLI. [*Raising her hand in a gesture of finality, and speaking with conviction*] I never eat immediately before using my voice. And you should not, either, Paula,—particularly candy. [*She moves across to the left to Mr. Ritter. She is an imposing woman, in her late fifties, with a wealth of false hair, perfectly done, and a martial bearing. She is one of those matrons who is frequently referred to in the suburban weeklies as a "leading spirit"; and this particular description has always so flattered Mrs. Pampinelli's particular vanity, that she overlooks no opportunity of justifying it: an effort that has resulted in a certain grandeur of voice and manner; which, rather fortunately, becomes the distinction of her person. She is gowned in sapphire-blue velvet, close-fitting, with an independent, triangular train, from the waist, probably four yards long. Her necklace, comb, the buckles on her black-velvet slippers, and her rings, are all touched with sapphire.*]

MRS. RITTER. [*Looking vaguely at the fudge-box*] There's so much of it here. [*Jenny appears from the left hallway.*]

MRS. P. and MRS. R., speaking together.

> MRS. P. [*Coming to Ritter's right*] Very tragic about poor Sheppard, wasn't it, Mr. Ritter?
>
> MRS. R. [*Going up to the center-door, and speaking to Jenny as she goes*] Mr. Spindler is answering the door, Jenny, you needn't bother.

RITTER and JENNY, speaking together.

> RITTER. [*To Mrs. Pampinelli*] Yes, it *was*—too bad.
>
> JENNY. [*To Mrs. Ritter*] Oh, all right, then. [*She withdraws, and Mrs. Ritter stands looking out into the right hallway.*]

MRS. PAMPINELLI. I suppose Paula wrote you.

RITTER. Yes.

MRS. PAMPINELLI. Dear me—I don't know when anything has so upset me. [*Ritter stands looking at the end of his cigar and Mrs. Pampinelli looks straight ahead.*] I don't believe I closed an eye the entire night,—wondering where on earth I should find someone to play his wife's part. [*Ritter glances at her, as he places the cigar in his mouth, and Mrs. Pampinelli looks at him quickly.*] Because, of course, you know that Mrs. Sheppard was to have played the part that Paula plays.

RITTER. Yes, so she told me. [*Mrs. Ritter, still nibbling at the fudge, wanders down and stands in the middle of the room.*]

MRS. PAMPINELLI. But we only had three days to get someone; and it didn't seem possible to me that anyone could memorize that part in that length of time. [*Mrs. Ritter touches her hair and makes a little sound of amusement,—a kind of modest acknowledgment of the brilliancy of her achievement.*] So I thought at first—of having Clara Sheppard go on anyway, and I should make an announcement; but, you see, Mr. Sheppard was buried on the fourteenth, and that was the night of the performance; and as I thought the matter over, it seemed to me that perhaps it was just a little too much to expect of her—[*Ritter gives her another glance.*] Considering her experience as an actress, I mean.

RITTER. [*Taking the cigar from his mouth and speaking with a shade of deliberation*] Couldn't she have kept his death a secret,—until after the performance?

MRS. PAMPINELLI. Well, I thought of that, too; [*Ritter looks at her steadily.*] but, you see, it was three days,—[*He nods, understandingly.*] and he was so very well known. [*She moves back across the room towards the table below the piano, and Ritter stands looking after her. Simultaneously, there is a frantic giggle from the right hallway. Mrs. Ritter goes up to the center-door, looks in the direction of the laughter, and waves her handkerchief, while Mrs. Pampinelli, passing below the table, gathers up her note-book and pencil and continues to the table below the casement-window, where she secures the manuscript. Ritter steps forward from his position before the mantelpiece, and disposes of some ashes on the little table-tray.*]

MRS. FELL. [*Out in the right hallway*] Paula, that's a very dangerous young man you have on that door tonight.

MRS. RITTER. [*Calling to her*] I think it's very kind of Mr. Spindler. [*Mrs. Pampinelli comes around in front of the big arm-chair below the casement-window.*]

MRS. FELL. [*Coming into view, with considerable flourish*] Kind! My dear, I haven't heard anything like it since I was twenty! [*She gives a little wave of her gorgeous, single white ostrich-plume fan at Mrs. Pampinelli.*] Hello, Betty! [*Then to Mrs. Ritter*] How are you, darling?

MRS. RITTER. Hello, Nelly. [*Nelly kisses her.*]

MRS. PAMPINELLI. [*Enthroning herself in the arm-chair at the right*] Is it *really* possible!

MRS. FELL. [*Turning from Mrs. Ritter and hurrying through the center-door*] You're a sweet child! [*Extending the fan towards Mrs. Pampinelli, and coming quickly forward to the table at the right below the piano*] Yes, and I should have been here every night at this hour if it weren't for that dreadful officer up at the parkway! [*She sets her fan and black-velvet bag on the table. Spindler comes in from the right hallway and engages in conversation with Mrs. Ritter in the centre-door.*] He seems to take a fiendish delight in selecting *my* car, of all the *millions* that pass there at this hour, to do *this*! [*She extends her right arm and hand, after the fashion of traffic-officers.*] So I told him yesterday afternoon, I said, "Look here, young man!" [*She points her forefinger as though reproving the officer.*] "You needn't expect any Christmas-present from *me* next Christmas, for you just—won't—get it. Not till you change your tactics." So he says, after this, he's just going to let me go ahead and run into a trolley-car;—see how I like that. [*Mrs. Pampinelli, making marginal notes in the manuscript, laughs faintly.*] "Well," I said, "it'd be a change, anyway,—from being stopped all the time." [*She abstractedly picks up her fan again.*] I don't think he likes my chauffeur. And I don't blame him; I don't like him myself. He drives too slow—[*She starts for the center-door.*] He's like an old woman. [*She sees Ritter, peering at her, and starts abruptly.*] Well, for Mercy's sake, Frederick Ritter, you don't mean to tell me that's you!

RITTER. I was here a minute ago.

MRS. FELL. [*Laughing flightily*] Well, I declare! I don't know what's happening to my eyes! [*Turning to Mrs. Pampinelli*] I saw him standing there, [*Turning back again and starting towards Ritter, with her hand extended*] but I thought it was one of the other gentlemen! How are you, dear boy? [*He takes her hand and stoops over as though to kiss her. She turns her head away quickly.*] Stop it! Frederick Ritter! [*Mrs. Pampinelli glances over, then resumes her notes. Mrs. Fell half-turns to Mrs. Ritter, who is still talking to Mr. Spindler up at the center-door.*] Paula!—do you see what this bad boy of yours is doing? [*Paula just looks and laughs meaninglessly, and resumes her conversation with Spindler.*] What brought you back so soon?

RITTER. [*Assuming the attitude and tone of a lover*] I got thinking of you.

MRS. FELL. [*Touching her hair*] I thought you were out in Seattle or South Carolina or one of those funny places.

RITTER. [*Leaning a bit closer and speaking more softly*] I couldn't keep away from you any longer. [*Nelly darts a swift glance at him.*]

MRS. FELL. [*Starting towards the right*] Don't play with fire, Frederick—[*He laughs hard. She pauses in the middle of the room and turns and looks at him.*] You know what they say about widows, and I've been all kinds. [*She continues over towards Mrs. Pampinelli.*] Oh, Professor Pampinelli! [*Turning and addressing Ritter directly*] I call her Professor, she knows so much. [*Turning back to Mrs. Pampinelli*] Mrs. P.

MRS. PAMPINELLI. [*Looking up suddenly*] I beg your pardon, Nelly dear—I didn't know you were speaking to me.

MRS. FELL. I want to know if you can take me home in your car tonight?

MRS. PAMPINELLI. Why, certainly, dear.

MRS. FELL. My chauffeur has been deviling me for the past two days about some boxing-bee,—or wrestling-match or something that he wants to see; and I told him he could go if there were someone here to take me home.

MRS. PAMPINELLI. I can take you, of course.

MRS. FELL. All right, then, I can chase him; [*She turns to the left.*] I won't hear any more about that. Oh, Mr. Spindler!

SPINDLER. Yes, mam? [*Excuses himself to Mrs. Ritter, who steps into the left hallway and beckons with her finger for Jenny.*]

MRS. FELL. Would you mind doing a favor for a very old lady?

SPINDLER. [*Who has hurried forward and is standing in the middle of the room, at attention.*] You know what I told you out at the door? [*Nelly gives a shriek, and giggles.*]

MRS. FELL. [*Looking coyly over Spindler's shoulder at Ritter*] Oh, you hear that, Frederick Ritter? You have a rival on the premises. Mr. Spindler told me out at the door tonight,—that *my* will was *his* pleasure.

RITTER. [*Looking at the tip of his cigar*] San Juan is never dead while Mr. Spindler lives. [*There is a general laugh.*]

SPINDLER. [*Turning to Ritter*] Say, that's pretty good!

MRS. FELL. Yes, I was afraid he was something of a gay deceiver.

SPINDLER. [*Speaking directly to Mrs. Fell*] Only one way to find out. [*Mrs. Fell laughs deprecatingly and sweeps the tip of her fan across his nose.*]

MRS. FELL. Naughty boy. [*She giggles a little more, then becomes practical.*] Well then, I'll tell you what you may do for me, Mr. Spindler, if you don't mind. [*Jenny appears in the left hallway and Mrs. Ritter gives her an order of some sort, which appears to require a bit of explanation.*] Go out to my chauffeur, [*She turns him round by the shoulder and they move up towards the center-door.*] you'll probably find him asleep in the car, and tell him I said it's all right,—he can go along—that Mrs. Pampinelli will take me home in *her* car.

SPINDLER. [*Hurrying out the right hallway*] Righto! [*Jenny withdraws.*]

MRS. FELL. [*Standing in the center-door and calling after him*] Like a good boy. [*She turns, to find Mrs. Ritter at her left in the center-door. She takes her arm and they come forward.*] Come in here, Paula Ritter, and explain to me *why* [*They stop in the middle of the room, just above the line on which Ritter is standing.*] you didn't tell me my—lover [*She peers around in front of Paula's shoulder at Ritter.*] was coming back today?

MRS. RITTER. [*Laughing faintly*] My dear, I didn't know it myself until twenty minutes ago.

MRS. FELL. [*Becoming instantly rigid, and piercing Mrs. Ritter with a look*] You don't mean to tell me he returned unexpectedly?

MRS. RITTER. He never even sent a wire.

MRS. FELL. [*Moving over to the right, to the little table below the piano*] I'm surprised at you, Frederick. I consider that the supreme indiscretion in a husband— [*She lays her fan down on the table.*] to return unexpectedly. Isn't it, Paula? [*She commences to unfasten her cloak.*]

MRS. RITTER. [*Moving over to help her*] I never got such a surprise in my life.

MRS. FELL. It has probably wrecked more perfectly good homes than any other one thing in the calendar. [*She slips her cloak off her shoulders, and Mrs. Ritter, who has passed back of her, takes it. It is a flowing affair in black and silver, with voluminous kimona sleeves edged with black fur, and a deep circular collar of silver-cloth and fur.*]

MRS. RITTER. I love your cape, Nelly.

MRS. FELL. [*Settling her ornaments*] Do you really?

MRS. RITTER. [*Examining it*] Beautiful.

MRS. PAMPINELLI. [*Reaching for it*] Let me see it, Paula.

MRS. RITTER. [*Handing it to her*] Where's your seal, Nelly?

MRS. FELL. I thought I wouldn't take it out this winter; I got so tired looking at it last year. I want to have that collar and cuffs taken off, anyway, before I wear it again;—there's too much skunk there.

MRS. PAMPINELLI. This is perfectly gorgeous, dear. [*To Mrs. Ritter*] Isn't it?

MRS. RITTER. [*Picking up Nelly's fan from the table*] Lovely. And isn't this sweet? [*Mrs. Pampinelli takes the fan from Mrs. Ritter and returns the wrap.*]

MRS. PAMPINELLI. Charming.

MRS. FELL. I'm so glad you like it;—I was afraid at first perhaps it might make me look a little too much like a bride.

RITTER. [*With mock derision*] Ha! [*Nelly snaps her head toward him and pins him with a narrow glare.*]

MRS. FELL. Don't be peevish, Frederick—

MRS. RITTER. [*To Mrs. Pampinelli, as she takes the fan from her and replaces it on the table*] Isn't he terrible!

MRS. FELL. It isn't my fault that your wife is a great actress. [*She gives a comic nod and wink at Mrs. Ritter. Ritter laughs.*]

MRS. RITTER. [*Starting towards the door up above the casement-window, at the right, with Mrs. Fell's cape*] Now, Fred Ritter, you just stop that!

MRS. PAMPINELLI. Never mind him, Paula—[*Paula goes out with the cape.*] He'll probably change his tune after tomorrow night. [*Mrs. Fell picks up her fan and commences to fan herself.*]

RITTER. [*Standing over above the table at the left, smoking*] I'm thinking of what happened to poor Jimmy Sheppard. [*Jenny comes in at the left hallway, carrying a small punch-bowl filled with claret, which she sets down carefully on the little stand in the hallway. Mrs. Ritter re-enters from the door on the right and crosses over to Jenny, whom she assists.*]

MRS. FELL. [*Strolling across towards Ritter, fanning herself*] Oh, I suppose it must be very difficult for the marvelous male, to suddenly find himself obliged to bask in the reflected glory of a mere wife. [*Mrs. Pampinelli laughs, over her notes.*] For I've never known one yet who was able to do it gracefully. [*She flips the tip of the fan at Ritter's nose. Mrs. Ritter gives Jenny a direction of some kind and Jenny goes out again at the left hallway.*]

MRS. PAMPINELLI. [*As Mrs. Fell saunters back again across the room*] Well, perhaps Mr. Ritter will show himself consistently *masculine* in this instance, and do the exceptional thing. [*Mrs. Ritter follows Jenny out.*]

RITTER. I suppose that's what you'd call *veiled* sarcasm, isn't it? [*Mrs. Pampinelli laughs and rises.*]

MRS. FELL. [*Standing in the middle of the room*] I shouldn't say it was veiled at *all*. [*Moving towards the table below the piano*] I don't think it's even *draped*.

MRS. PAMPINELLI. [*Laughing still, and coming to the little table*] Here's the manuscript, Nelly.

MRS. FELL. [*Stepping closer to the table*] Yes, dear.

RITTER. What are you going to do now, keep *on* giving this show?

MRS. PAMPINELLI. Well, not this particular one, Mr. Ritter, no; but we are going to continue giving shows.

RITTER. What's the idea?

MRS. FELL. They're to be for different charities.

MRS. PAMPINELLI. And then they will afford the boys and girls an opportunity of developing themselves as artists.

RITTER. What are they going to do, all go on the stage?

MRS. PAMPINELLI. Well, hardly all of them will go;—but those that we feel have sufficient talent we will encourage to go on, by all means.

RITTER. Do you think Mrs. Ritter has sufficient talent?

MRS. FELL. She's wonderful, Fred, really.

MRS. PAMPINELLI. Yes, I should say that Paula had a very remarkable talent.

RITTER. Well, what will you do about *her*?

MRS. PAMPINELLI. How do you mean, Mr. Ritter, what will we *do* about her?

RITTER. Why, I mean,—you'd hardly encourage *her* to go on the stage, would you?

MRS. PAMPINELLI. And why not?

RITTER. Why, what about her home? [*Nelly Fell touches her hair and gives Mrs. Pampinelli a look of amused impatience.*] She couldn't very well walk away and leave that, could she?

MRS. PAMPINELLI. Well, personally, Mr. Ritter, I have always felt that, where it is a question of talent, one should not allow himself to be deterred by purely personal considerations.

MRS. FELL. She's really awfully good, Fred! You wait till you see—You'll want her to go yourself.

RITTER. [*Stepping quietly to the table at the left and disposing of some cigar-ashes*] She'll have to be pretty good.

MRS. FELL. Won't he, Betty?

MRS. PAMPINELLI. Well, as far as that is concerned, I think that the question of whether to be or or not to be an actress, is one that every woman must, at some time or other in her life, decide for herself. [*Spindler hurries in from the right hallway and down to Mrs. Fell's left, where he stands at attention, saluting, of course, as usual. Mr. Spindler is full of salutes. He was in the army;—drafted ten weeks before the armistice; and subjected throughout the long term of his service to the dangers and exposure of a clerkship in the Personnel at Upton. And he's never gotten over it; being of that immature type of mind upon which the letter of the Military makes a profound impression. He's a peppy person, thin and stilted,—in dinner clothes,—with sleek hair and goggle glasses: one of that distressing student-order that is inevitably to be found in the retinue of some Mrs. Pampinelli,—her social status and constant championship of so-called artistic movements affording him a legitimate indulgence of his particular weaknesses. So he becomes a kind of lead-pencil-bearer extraordinary to her ladyship; and her ladyship tolerates him,—for a variety of reasons; not the least of which is his unfailing attitude of acquiescence in all her opinions. And she has so many opinions,—and on so many different subjects, that this feature of Mr. Spindler's disposition is far from inconsiderable. Then, he has a most highly developed faculty for small correctnesses,—an especially valuable asset, in view of the enormous amount of detail work incidental to Mrs. Pampinelli's vast activities. He reminds her of things, or, "brings them to her attention," as she puts it. For Mr. Spindler is one of those—fortunately few—people who remembers things—word for word—even the things he's read—And he appears to have read most everything. And he quotes incessantly. As Mrs. Pampinelli has already observed of him, "he is one of those rare persons who never forsakes one in the hour of quotation."]* Look here, Nelly.

MRS. FELL. Yes, dear. [*Mrs. Ritter comes in from the left hallway carrying several punch-glasses, which she puts down on the hallway table.*]

MRS. PAMPINELLI. [*Indicating a certain line in the manuscript with her lead-pencil*] There are a couple of little changes here on page twelve—[*Mrs. Fell opens her lorgnon and looks at the manuscript.*] I have them marked.

MRS. FELL. [*Becoming conscious of Spindler at her left*] Pardon me, Betty. [*Turning to Spindler*] Did you tell him, Mr. Spindler?

SPINDLER. Yes, mam; he's gone on his way rejoicing.

MRS. FELL. You're a sweet child.

SPINDLER. [*Snapping his salute*] Thank you. [*He does an about-face and goes up to Mrs. Ritter,—Ritter watching him with an expression susceptible of infinite interpretation.*]

MRS. FELL. The only man I've met in a long time that has made me wish I were—ten years younger.

RITTER. Ha!

MRS. FELL. [*Pertly*] Outside of you, of course.

MRS. PAMPINELLI. [*With a touch of wearied impatience*] Look here, dear.

MRS. FELL. [*Stepping quickly to the table again and re-adjusting her lorgnon*] Yes, I beg your pardon.

MRS. PAMPINELLI. You see, in this line here,—the author has employed a defective verb in the perfect tense. [*Mrs. Fell looks suddenly at her and then right back to the manuscript again. Ritter is watching them closely.*] Would you come here for a moment, Mr. Spindler?

SPINDLER. Certainly, certainly. [*Excuses himself to Mrs. Ritter, with whom he has been chatting, and comes down briskly to Mrs. Fell's left.*]

MRS. PAMPINELLI. If you please.

MRS. FELL. [*Appearing to have some difficulty locating the defective verb*] Where is that, now, that you were saying, Betty?

MRS. PAMPINELLI. [*Indicating with the point of the pencil*] Right there, dear. [*Nelly just looks at the spot, through her lorgnon.*] This is the point I was speaking to you about last night, Mr. Spindler.

SPINDLER. [*Securing his goggles*] Oh, yes, yes! [*Ritter draws Mrs. Ritter's attention to the group down at the table. She reproves him with a steady stare. He smiles and shakes his head hopelessly.*]

MRS. PAMPINELLI. You see, this author has employed a defective here, in the perfect tense.

SPINDLER. [*Looking closely*] Ah, yes, I see.

MRS. PAMPINELLI. [*Looking at him directly*] So I have changed it. [*He straightens up and looks at her, and Mrs. Fell looks from one to the other.*]

SPINDLER. A very good change. [*He nods and crosses over to the left, passing below the table at the left. Ritter watches him until he takes up his position just below the mantelpiece, rather ill at ease under Ritter's gaze.*]

MRS. PAMPINELLI. I think so. So, if you'll just watch that Nelly. [*She picks up the manuscript.*]

MRS. FELL. All right, I'll watch it. [*She reaches for her bag and takes out a lip-stick. Jenny appears from the left hallway with a tray of cakes, which Mrs. Ritter assists her in making room for on the hall table.*]

MRS. PAMPINELLI. [*Starting for the center-door*] I must show it to Paula, it's her line. [*The door-bell rings.*] Paula child. [*Jenny passes back of Mrs. Ritter and goes out into the right hallway to answer the door-bell.*]

MRS. RITTER. [*Eating a cake*] Yes, dear? [*Mrs. Pampinelli calls her attention to the change in the manuscript. Mrs. Fell is making up her lips down at the table below the piano. Ritter is watching her, and Spindler is watching Ritter, and trying to assume his general deportment.*]

RITTER. Are *you* in the show, Nelly?

MRS. FELL. [*Without turning, and applying the lip-stick, with the aid of the little mirror in her hand-bag*] Who, me?

RITTER. Yes.

MRS. FELL. [*Half-turning, and giving him a melting look*] Yes;—I play a chicken. [*She returns to her mirror.*]

RITTER. [*Casually*] In the last act, I suppose. [*Nelly snaps her head around and pierces him with one of her looks.*]

MRS. FELL. No, and not in the last stages, either. [*She resumes her make-up. Nelly is forever making up. But, she does know how to do it. Of course, she should, considering the years of her experience in the art. For Nelly Fell's age amounts to an achievement; one of those attainments so absolutely undisputed that it is perfectly permissible to refer to it in any gathering. She says she'll "soon be sixty"; but the short and simple annals of society record flutterings of the lady as far back as the first term of President Grant. And she's still fluttering—a perennial ingenue, full of brittle moves and staccato vocalisms. She looks like a little French marquise, so chic, and twittery—and rich. For, of course, Nelly is wealthy—enormously so; it would be utterly impossible to have her hair and not have money; the feature is financial in itself; so silver-white, with a lovely bandau of small, pale-pink leaves, tipped with diamond dewdrops; all heightened tremendously by the creation in black velvet she is wearing. This gown is heavily trimmed with silver, and quite sleeveless, with two panels of the goods fastened at the waist on either side and trailing at least a yard. She has a preference for diamonds and pearls, obviously, for her ear-rings, dog-collar, bracelets and rings are all of those gems, and her long, triple-string necklace is of pearls. Altogether, Nelly is a very gorgeous little old lady—from the topmost ringlet of her aristocratic hair, to the pearl buckles on her tiny black-velvet slippers.*]

SPINDLER. Mrs. Fell is the official promptress.

MRS. FELL. [*Turning her head and looking at Ritter*] I *prompt* everybody. [*She replaces her lip-stick in the hand-bag.*]

RITTER. Yes?

MRS. FELL. [*Putting the hand-bag down again on the table*] As well as lending my moral support.

RITTER. Yes? [*Spindler laughs.*]

MRS. FELL. [*To Ritter*] You bold thing!

HOSSEFROSSE. [*Coming into view from the right hallway*] Good evening, everybody!

MRS. PAMPINELLI. [*Turning to him, from Mrs. Ritter, with whom she has been discussing the change in the manuscript*] Oh, good evening, Mr. Hossefrosse. [*They shake hands.*]

MRS. RITTER. Mr. Hossefrosse. [*Mrs. Pampinelli comes forward into the room again, bringing the manuscript with her.*]

HOSSEFROSSE. Mrs. Ritter—good evening. [*Mrs. Ritter asks him if he will have a glass of claret and he says yes, so she proceeds to fill him out one.*]

MRS. PAMPINELLI. I hope the rest of the people aren't far behind you.

HOSSEFROSSE. Are we late?

MRS. FELL. [*Waving to him*] Hello, Huxley.

MRS. PAMPINELLI. Not very.

HOSSEFROSSE. Hello, Nelly. How are you? [*Mrs. Ritter gives him the claret, and he stands up at the center-door with her, drinking it. Teddy Spearing wanders in from the right hallway.*]

MRS. PAMPINELLI. [*Passing below the little table below the piano and laying the manuscript on it*] Here's the manuscript, Nelly. [*She continues to the arm-chair below the casement-window, and, picking up her note-book from the little table at her right, sits down and commences to make notes.*]

MRS. FELL. [*Seeing Teddy Spearing, and starting towards the right partition*] Oh, Teddy Spearing!

TEDDY. Hello, Nelly.

MRS. FELL. [*Beckoning him with her fan*] Come here, dear, I've got something to tell you. [*Teddy leans over the partition at the right and Nelly kneels on the partition-seat and whispers something to him. Hossefrosse and Mrs. Ritter are conversing in the center-door, Mrs. Pampinelli is making notes down at the right, Ritter is standing over in front of the mantelpiece, smoking, and Spindler is standing just below him, to his left, watching him.*]

SPINDLER. [*In a sudden surge of courage, and taking a rather nonchalant step towards Ritter*] Could you spare one of those cigars, please? [*Ritter looks at him keenly, then reaches in his vest-pocket for a cigar.*]

RITTER. Do you smoke?

SPINDLER. Semi-occasionally, yes. [*Ritter hands him the cigar and he steps nonchalantly back to his former position, Ritter keeping one eye on him. He examines the cigar curiously, and, being apparently very near-sighted, seems to have considerable difficulty in deciphering the band-inscription.*]

RITTER. You can light *either* end of it.

SPINDLER. [*Very self-conscious*] Yes,—I was just looking at this label here: it's rather keen. [*He puts the cigar in his mouth, and attempts an attitude of careless detachment.*]

RITTER. Have you got a match?

SPINDLER. I don't—[*As he opens his mouth to speak the cigar falls on the floor, and he scrambles after it.*]

TEDDY. [*Laughing incredulously and turning away from Nelly*] Oh, Nelly!

MRS. FELL. Upon my word, dear! Come here till I tell you. [*Teddy returns to the partition and Nelly proceeds with her gossip.*]

SPINDLER. [*Straightening up, and attempting another man-of-the-world attitude*] I don't care to smoke just now, thank you. [*He holds the cigar in his fingers.*]

RITTER. [*As things settle again*] You've been in the army, haven't you?

SPINDLER. [*Turning to Ritter with a suggestion of military erectness*] Yes; I put in the better part of three months down at Upton, in the Personnel.

RITTER. I imagined from your salute you'd been around one of the camps.

SPINDLER. Yes,—I was Third Lieutenant down there—[*Ritter looks at him sharply; then Spindler turns and meets the look.*] Regimental Sergeant Major.

RITTER. Rest.

MRS. FELL. [*Coming away from the partition*] So I'm going to ask him right out the very next time I meet him. [*She comes down to the little table below the piano again. Mr. Hossefrosse comes through the center-door towards Ritter, rubbing his hands, and Teddy moves over towards Mrs. Ritter, who is still officiating at the punch-bowl.*]

TEDDY and HOSSEFROSSE, speaking together.

> TEDDY. [*Speaking to Mrs. Fell*] Maybe he doesn't know it himself.
>
> HOSSEFROSSE. [*Addressing Ritter*] Ah, Mr. Ritter! How do you do, sir? [*They shake hands.*]

RITTER. How do you do?

MRS. FELL and HOSSEFROSSE, together.

> MRS. FELL. Well, I'm going to find out, whether he does or not.
>
> HOSSEFROSSE. [*To Ritter*] Decided there was no place like home, eh? [*He laughs, with a mirthless effusiveness.*]

RITTER. Are you in the show, too? [*Mrs. Ritter fills out a glass of claret for Teddy.*]

MRS. FELL and HOSSEFROSSE, together.

> MRS. FELL. I should say he is in it.

HOSSEFROSSE. We're all in it.

MRS. FELL. He's the leading man. [*Hossefrosse raises his right hand toward Nelly and laughs deprecatingly.*] Unfortunately, there isn't a place in the play where he can use that perfectly gorgeous singing-voice of his. [*Hossefrosse is quite overcome, and crosses, with hand extended, to Spindler.*] It's true.

HOSSEFROSSE. Good evening, Mr. Spindler.

SPINDLER. Good evening, good evening. [*In shifting the cigar from his right hand to his left he drops it.*]

HOSSEFROSSE. Uh! I beg your pardon! [*Mrs. Ritter laughs at something Teddy has said to her, then hands him a glass of claret. Mr. Hossefrosse stoops to pick up Spindler's cigar.*]

SPINDLER. [*Stooping also, after the cigar*] That's all right.

HOSSEFROSSE and SPINDLER, together.

> HOSSEFROSSE. I'll get it. [*He picks it up and hands it to Spindler.*]
>
> SPINDLER. It isn't lit.

HOSSEFROSSE. There we are.

SPINDLER. Thank you very much.

HOSSEFROSSE. Don't mention it. [*He crosses down to Nelly, who is looking through the manuscript at the table below the piano.*]

TEDDY. [*Coming through the center-door and speaking to Ritter*] How do you do, Mr. Ritter?

RITTER. [*Shaking hands with him*] How are you?

TEDDY. [*Nodding to Spindler*] Good evening.

SPINDLER. Good evening, sir; good evening.

MRS. PAMPINELLI. Teddy!

TEDDY. [*Crossing towards the piano*] Yes?

MRS. RITTER, MRS. PAMPINELLI and HOSSEFROSSE, together.

> MRS. RITTER. [*Waving her handkerchief toward the right hallway*] Hello, Florence!
>
> MRS. PAMPINELLI. [*Addressing Teddy*] Did you telephone that man about those tickets?

HOSSEFROSSE. [*Standing at Mrs. Fell's left shoulder*] What are you doing, Nelly?

FLORENCE, MRS. FELL and TEDDY, together.

> FLORENCE. [*Out in the right hallway*] Am I the last? [*She hurries into view and whispers something to Paula at the center-door which sends Paula into a fit of laughing.*]

> MRS. FELL. [*To Hossefrosse*] Making more changes. [*He crosses over to the right in front of Nelly and sits on the piano-stool, back of Mrs. Pampinelli.*]

> TEDDY. [*Answering Mrs. Pampinelli*] Yes, I did, Mrs. Pampinelli, he said he'd have them there all right.

MRS. PAMPINELLI. Thank you so much. [*Teddy goes up and crosses above the piano, where he engages Mr. Hossefrosse in conversation.*] Hello, Florence! [*Jenny comes into view from the right hallway.*]

FLORENCE. [*Coming straight forward from the center-door*] Am I the last? [*The front door-bell rings again, and Jenny turns and goes back into the right hallway again.*]

MRS. PAMPINELLI. No, but you're very close to it. How are you, dear?

FLORENCE. Rushed like mad. [*Flipping her lynx muff*] Hello, everybody. Hello, Nelly. [*She swings round to her left.*]

MRS. FELL. Hello, Flossie.

FLORENCE. How do you do, Mr. Spindler? [*Hossefrosse gets up and whispers something to Mrs. Pampinelli, in which she agrees.*]

SPINDLER. How do you do? [*Ritter bows very graciously to Florence, and Mrs. Ritter comes forward to her husband's right, eating a piece of cake.*]

FLORENCE. [*Extending the muff at arms-length at Ritter*] No, I don't speak to you at all. [*She removes her stole.*]

RITTER. What's the matter?

FLORENCE. Paula, did you know your husband is becoming very snooty? [*Hossefrosse resumes his seat on the piano-stool.*]

MRS. RITTER. [*Sliding her hand through Ritter's right arm*] Why didn't you speak to Florence at the station today, Fred?

RITTER. I didn't see you today.

FLORENCE. Well, my dear, you *must* be getting old; for Irene Colter and I did everything but stand on our heads to attract your attention. [*On the last word of this sentence she flips one of the tails of the stole at him, and he ducks, as though afraid*

- 34 -

of getting hurt.] Where shall I put these, Paula? [*Mrs. Pampinelli rises quietly from her chair at the right, and, lost in thought, proceeds slowly and majestically across in front of Mrs. Fell to the middle of the room, tapping her lead-pencil on the note-book.*]

MRS. RITTER. I'll take them. [*She takes the muff and stole from Florence and goes up and out into the right hallway with them.*]

FLORENCE. [*Espying Teddy up back of the piano, shading his eyes with his hand, as though trying to see her from a great distance*] Hello, Teddy dear! [*Goes towards him*] What are you doing away back here in the corner? [*She makes a sudden move as though to tickle him in the ribs, but he laughs and jumps away. Mrs. Pampinelli has by this time reached the center of the room, where she stands turning from side to side in a profound indecision as to the relationship of certain positions. She indicates her line of thought by divers pointings and flippings of the lead-pencil. Ritter watches her with narrow amusement; and, presently, Mrs. Fell, who is still occupied with the manuscript at the little table, looks up, distracted by the gyrations of the lead-pencil.*]

MRS. FELL. What's the matter, Betty?

MRS. PAMPINELLI. I was just wondering about a little piece of business here.

SPINDLER. [*Stepping to the back of the arm-chair at the left and leaning over it towards Mrs. Pampinelli*] Can I help you, Mrs. P.?

MRS. PAMPINELLI. [*Without turning to him*] No, thank you; it's purely technical. [*He resumes his position at the left corner of the mantelpiece and glances at Ritter, who is obliged to use his handkerchief to hide his amusement. Mrs. Ritter comes in through the door at the right, above the piano.*]

MRS. FELL. Betty, did I tell you I saw Clara Sheppard today? [*But Mrs. Pampinelli is still deep in technical profundities, and simply silences her with a gesture of her right hand.*]

MRS. RITTER. [*Coming forward at the right of the piano*] Where did you see her, Nelly?

MRS. FELL. Darlington's, at the mourning counter.

MRS. PAMPINELLI. [*Coming suddenly out of her abstraction, and turning to Mrs. Fell*] Is she going in black?

MRS. FELL. My dear, she's *in* it already.

TWILLER. [*Coming in the right hallway*] Good evening!

MRS. PAMPINELLI. She's very foolish, under the circumstances.

MRS. FELL. That's just what I told her today.

TWILLER. [*Coming through the center-door and forward at the left of the piano*] Good evening, Mrs. Ritter.

MRS. RITTER. Good evening, Mr. Twiller.

TWILLER. [*To Hossefrosse, casually*] Huxley.

HOSSEFROSSE. [*Shifting from the piano-stool to the arm-chair, which Mrs. Pampinelli has just vacated, and proceeding to study his part, which he has taken from his pocket*] Hello, Ralph.

MRS. FELL. Hello, Ralph.

TWILLER. Nelly!

MRS. PAMPINELLI. [*Still in the middle of the room*] You're the ten o'clock scholar again tonight, Mr. Twiller. [*Jenny crosses from the right hallway to the left, and goes out.*]

TWILLER. I'm awfully sorry, Mrs. P., really; but the fates seem to be against me. [*Teddy gives a little whistle at him. He turns and sees him, standing with Florence, up back of the piano.*] Hello, Teddy! [*He goes towards him, and Teddy shoots at him with his thumb and forefinger, by way of reply. Florence smiles and extends her left arm and hand towards him.*]

MRS. PAMPINELLI and TWILLER, together.

> MRS. PAMPINELLI. [*Moving over from the middle of the room to the left of Mrs. Fell, who is still at the table below the piano*] What was that you were saying, Nelly, about Clara Sheppard?
>
> TWILLER. Flossie, dear, I didn't see you two up here! [*He takes Florence's hand and kisses it. Then he crosses to the left and shakes hands with Ritter; then over to Spindler, and then starts back towards Florence, at the piano. As he passes Ritter, Ritter taps him on the right shoulder; he turns, and Ritter asks him something. He replies, and they stand chatting for a moment; then Ritter indicates the partition-seat behind them and they sit down, to talk it over.*]

MRS. FELL. Why, I simply told her—I said, "Don't be spectacular, dear; it'll only make it more difficult for you when you want to marry again. And," I said, "you probably *will* marry again,"—[*Spindler sits on the chair below the door at the left.*]

MRS. PAMPINELLI. Of course she will.

MRS. FELL. "For you're a comparatively young woman. So," I said, "just get through the next few months as undramatically as possible. [*Jenny enters in the left hallway and takes empty glasses off.*] I know he was your *first* husband, and all that; but, after all," I said, "he was *only* your husband: it isn't as though you'd lost someone who was very *close* to you"—[*She turns her head and speaks directly to Mrs. Pampinelli.*] Like one of your own people, [*Turning to Mrs. Ritter, who is standing at her right*] or something like that, I mean. "And," I said, "another thing, darling,—*always remember*—he'd have very soon put another in *your* place if it had been you." [*She finishes the remark to Mrs. Pampinelli.*]

MRS. PAMPINELLI. [*Knowingly, and with conviction*] I should say he would.

MRS. FELL. [*Reaching for her hand-bag*] And I felt like saying, "And I could give you the names and addresses right now of *several* that he would have put in your place *long ago*, only for the law."

MRS. PAMPINELLI. [*With a shade of confidence*] She must have known it.

MRS. FELL. [*Reflecting the tone*] Of *course*, she knew it. [*Florence leaves Teddy, up at the piano, and crosses to Ritter and Twiller, to show them a piece of music. They rise, and she indicates a certain point on the sheet; then she continues down to Spindler, who rises at her approach, and shows it to him.*]

MRS. RITTER. How is she, Nelly?

MRS. FELL. My dear, she looks a perfect wreck. [*Florence sits on the arm of the arm-chair at the left and Spindler resumes the little chair below the left door, and drawing it a bit closer to the arm-chair. He appears to be telling Florence something very interesting.*]

MRS. RITTER. Poor soul.

MRS. FELL. She says no one will *ever* know how she feels—about losing that part. And she says she simply cannot *wait* until tomorrow night, [*She turns to Mrs. Pampinelli.*] to see Paula's interpretation of it. [*Mrs. Ritter gives an inane little laugh, and Mrs. Fell turns quickly to her.*] She's heard so much about it. [*Jenny comes in from the left hallway again with fresh glasses. She sets them down on the hallway table and proceeds to arrange them.*]

MRS. PAMPINELLI. Is she coming to the performance tomorrow night?

MRS. FELL. She says she'll see that performance, if she has to disguise herself.

MRS. RITTER. Doesn't that sound just like her? [*Nelly nods agreement.*]

MRS. PAMPINELLI. Yes,—she's so full of dramatic instinct.

MRS. FELL. [*With a touch of bitterness*] He never appreciated it though.

MRS. PAMPINELLI. My dear, has *any* artist *ever* been adequately appreciated?

MRS. RITTER. I understand he was very heavily insured.

MRS. FELL. Oh, yes!

MRS. PAMPINELLI. She *seemed* very optimistic when I spoke to her on the telephone.

MRS. FELL. I believe your husband's company had him insured for quite a lot, didn't they, Paula?

MRS. RITTER. [*Lowering her tone*] I believe they did, Nelly,—but I couldn't say for just how much.

MRS. FELL. [*Quietly detaching herself*] I must find that out. [*She passes back of Mrs. Pampinelli and across towards Ritter. Mrs. Ritter and Mrs. Pampinelli continue in conversation.*] Frederick, I want to ask you something. [*He steps forward, excusing himself to Twiller.*] Pardon me, Ralph.

TWILLER. That's all right, Nelly. [*He crosses again to Teddy.*]

MRS. FELL. Frederick, what did you think when you heard Jimmy Sheppard was dead?

RITTER. Why, I thought he was dead, of course. [*Mrs. Ritter leaves Mrs. Pampinelli, passing back of her, and goes up to assist Jenny with her arrangements. Mrs. Pampinelli busies herself with making notations on the margin of the manuscript, at the little table.*]

MRS. FELL. [*Flipping the tip of her fan in his face*] Oh, did you, Smarty! [*Ritter raises his right hand, as though to ward off the blow.*] Well, listen, Frederick. [*He attends, and she becomes confidential.*] He left quite a bit of insurance, didn't he?

RITTER. Yes—about three hundred thousand, I believe.

MRS. FELL. [*Becoming generally stoney*] Is there a will, do you know?

RITTER. I don't know; I suppose there is.

MRS. FELL. Well, I hope she was sharp enough to see that there is. Because if there isn't, you know, she's only entitled to a third in this state. That's all the widow's entitled to. And, you know, Frederick, Clara Sheppard could never in this world get along on a bare hundred thousand dollars; you know that as well as I do.

RITTER. Well, she has quite a bit of money of her own, hasn't she?

MRS. FELL. Oh, tons of it, yes; but there's no sense in using her own if she can use his. [*Ritter glances at her, but she has turned away slightly to cough, behind her fan. Jenny goes out at the left hallway.*] Was sudden, wasn't it?

RITTER. Yes, it was.

MRS. FELL. We were terribly inconvenienced. Because I'd simply *deluged* my friends with tickets. [*Mrs. Ritter is up at the punch-bowl, sampling the punch and nibbling at the cakes.*]

RITTER. I can't understand why you didn't postpone the show.

MRS. FELL. That's what *I* wanted to do; but Mrs. P. here was superstitious.

MRS. PAMPINELLI. [*Catching her name, and straightening up from the manuscript, imperiously*] What are you saying about Mrs. P., Nelly Fell?

MRS. FELL. Why, Frederick was wondering why we didn't postpone the performance when Jimmy Sheppard died,—and *I* told him you were superstitious about a postponement.

MRS. PAMPINELLI. No, Nelly, I was not superstitious, so please don't say that I was; I shouldn't care to have such an impression get abroad.

MRS. FELL. [*Touching her hair*] Well, you were something, Betty.

MRS. PAMPINELLI. Yes, Nelly, I admit that I was something,—but it was not superstitious. I was,—[*She looks out and away off, and feels for the word.*] intuitive. [*She turns her head and looks directly at Ritter, who drops his eyes to the tip of his cigar. Nelly Fell, following Mrs. Pampinelli's eyes, looks at Ritter also. Then everyone's eyes shift to Mrs. Pampinelli. Florence turns languidly and looks; and Mrs. Ritter, with a glass of punch in one hand, and a small cake in the other, moves forward, in the middle of the room, and stands looking and listening—and chewing. Hossefrosse steps over to the table behind which Mrs. Pampinelli is standing, and takes the manuscript,—returning with it to the arm-chair, and becoming absorbed in a comparison of a certain page of it with his individual part.*] I have struggled so long to inaugurate a Little Theatre Movement in this community, that I had intuitively anticipated the occurrence of some obstacle to thwart me; so that, when the telephone-bell rang, on the night of Mr. Sheppard's death, I said to myself, before I even took down the receiver, [*She plants her lead-pencil on the table and assumes something of the aspect of a crusader.*] "*This* is my event. Something has happened—that is going to put my sincerity in this movement to the test. And I must remember, as Mr. Lincoln said at Gettysburg, 'It is better that we should perish, than that those ideals for which we struggle should perish.'" [*She turns her gaze in the direction of Ritter, but Mrs. Ritter is first in the line of vision, with her eyes full of the coast of Greenland, and her mouth full of cake. As she becomes suddenly conscious that Mrs. Pampinelli has stopped talking and is looking directly at her, she meets the look and breaks into an utterly irrelevant little laugh.*]

RITTER. It's a singular thing, but I've noticed that invariably there's a *fatality* connected with these amateur performances.

MRS. PAMPINELLI. Unfortunately, that is true, Mr. Ritter, I agree with you. But then, we are not dismayed; we have the lessons of history to fortify us; for whenever the torch of essential culture has been raised, [*She raises the lead-pencil as though it were a torch.*] there has unfailingly been the concomitant exactment of a human life. [*She stands holding the torch aloft until the little cuckoo-clock over the door at the left cuckoos the half-hour. Ritter looks at it, and Nelly Fell gives it a glance. Florence, too, turns and looks up. Then Mrs. Pampinelli turns her eyes slowly upon it and withers it with a look.*] Well, children, it's eight-thirty,—[*She gathers up her train and tosses it across her left arm, then comes around to the right in front of the table where she has been standing. Mrs. Ritter returns to the table in the hallway and sets down her empty glass. Ritter goes up after her and she fills him out a drink. Florence rises from the arm of the chair, and, passing in front of the table at the left, goes up and across back of the piano and out the door, at the right. As she passes above the piano she says something to Teddy, who has come down at the right of the piano, from his late position up near the door, and is crossing below it. Twiller turns and goes out through the center-door and stands leaning over the partition in the right hallway. Hossefrosse rises, settles his clothes and clears his throat. Mr. Spindler, also, has risen, and is replacing his chair back against the wall, below the door.*] Time we went "unto the breach" once more.

MRS. FELL. [*Stepping forward a little to the center of the room, and stretching her hand towards Mr. Hossefrosse*] You have my props, Huxley.

HOSSEFROSSE. [*Crossing below the table, to give her the manuscript*] I beg your pardon, Nelly; I was just looking at something here.

MRS. FELL. Thanks. [*She pulls him towards her and whispers something.*]

MRS. PAMPINELLI. [*Standing at the left of the little table*] Have you my other pencil, Mr. Spindler?

SPINDLER. [*Hurrying across towards her*] I believe you left it over here on this little table. [*He passes below Teddy, who is just crossing to the left, and continues on between the piano and the table to the little table below the casement-window. Nelly Fell breaks into a shrill giggle, pushes Hossefrosse towards the center-door, and crosses to the left, passing below the table. She is in a violent state of laughter. Hossefrosse goes on up to the center-door, and, excusing himself to Ritter, who is standing there drinking, passes out into the right hallway. Teddy comes around back of the arm-chair at the left and sits in the arm-chair. Mrs. Pampinelli has moved to the right of the table below the piano, where she stands reviewing her notes.*]

MRS. FELL. [*To Teddy, confidentially, as she takes up her position on the chair below the door at the left*] I'll tell you later. [*She sits down.*]

MRS. PAMPINELLI. [*Tapping her lead-pencil on the table and addressing them generally*] Now, folks,—[*Ritter sets his glass on the table and steps into the right hallway, where he converses with Twiller for a second, then stands listening; while Mrs. Ritter hurries in and settles herself on the partition-seat at the left and listens attentively.*] you understand, of course, that the setting will be just as it was at the Civic Club on the fourteenth; only, of course, as you know, the stage at Hutchy Kutchy is considerably larger. That, however, need not concern us particularly, as the entrances and exits will be relatively the same. [*She finishes this speech to Mr. Spindler, who is standing at her right, waiting for her to take the lead-pencil.*] Oh, thank you, Mr. Spindler. [*She gives him the one she has—simply an exchange of pencils, and he salutes and returns to a position below the casement-window. Florence comes in at the right door again, wearing her furs, and comes down at the right of the piano. Mrs. Pampinelli moves a little towards the center-door.*] Are you going to watch the rehearsal, Mr. Ritter?

MRS. FELL. Of course, he is!

RITTER. [*Coming through the center-door*] If I wouldn't be in the way.

MRS. PAMPINELLI. Not at all,—very glad to have you.

MRS. FELL. He can sit over here with the promptress. [*He crosses towards Nelly, picking up the little chair above the table at the left, as he passes. Hossefrosse emerges from the right hallway carrying a light, soft hat, a cane and gloves, and stands in the center-door. Florence steps across below the piano and asks Mrs. Pampinelli something.*] If you can behave yourself. [*Florence returns to the corner of the piano nearest the window and drapes herself on it. She's a very gorgeous-looking thing, in a sleeveless gown of canary-colored metallic silk, made quite daringly severe, to exploit the long, lithe lines of her greyhound figure. There's a chain-effect girdle with the dress, of vivid jade, worn loose, and an ornament of the same jade on the left shoulder, from which the goods falls in a plain drape down in front of the arm to the bottom of the skirt. She has a perfect shock of hair,—rather striking,—a kind of suspicious auburn; and she has it bobbed. Her slippers and stockings are white.*]

MRS. PAMPINELLI. You needn't sit there yet, Teddy, I'm going to run through the last scene first,—

TEDDY. [*Rising*] Oh, all right.

MRS. PAMPINELLI. For Mr. Hossefrosse's lines. [*Teddy passes in front of the table at the left and goes up to the center-door and out into the right hallway, where he chats with Twiller and watches the proceedings over the partition. Spindler comes over and asks Mrs. Pampinelli something. Ritter places his chair beside Nelly's, above it, and sits down, assuming the attitude of a lover.*]

MRS. FELL. [*Pushing Ritter's arm away*] Stop it, Frederick Ritter! Paula! [*Spindler returns to his post.*]

MRS. RITTER. [*Inanely*] Behave yourself, Fred.

MRS. PAMPINELLI. Now, folks,—[*She moves slowly down and across towards the table at the left.*] Mr. Spindler will attend to the various cues tonight, and at the performance tomorrow night as well. [*Speaking directly to Nelly*] So we won't have to bother about that. [*Turning round to her left and addressing the others*] He will do all the rapping. [*She raps a little.*] And he has a little telephone-bell of his own, [*She moves across again towards the back of the table at the right.*] which he has very kindly tendered the use of. Have you that bell with you tonight, Mr. Spindler? [*He holds out a bell and battery arrangement on a piece of wood, having taken it from his pocket immediately she referred to it, and rings it twice.*] Splendid. [*She passes above the table and comes forward at the right of it, very thoughtfully.*] That's splendid. [*Spindler replaces the battery.*] Now, children,—[*She crosses in front of the table.*] I think, first, I should like to take that scene at the finish, between Doctor Arlington and his wife; [*She is standing at the left of the table, speaking directly to Hossefrosse, who is standing in the center-door, with his hat on, at a rather absurd angle, and holding his cane in one hand and his gloves in the other, in a very stilted fashion. Hossefrosse is a terribly well-fed-looking person in dinner clothes, perhaps, thirty-eight years of age,—flamingly florid of complexion, and with an effusiveness of manner that is probably only saved from absolute effervescence by the ponderous counterpoise of his dignity.*] there are a few little things in there I want to correct. [*Crossing over back of the table at the left towards Mrs. Fell*] Page eighteen or nineteen, I think it is, Nelly. It's the scene at the finish between Mr. Hossefrosse and Miss McCrickett. [*Nelly looks for the place, through her lorgnon.*] Oh! [*Mrs. Pampinelli turns back to the others again.*] and one thing more I want to mention, boys and girls, before I forget it. [*She takes a funny little coughing spell.*] Pardon me. [*She coughs again.*] Oh, dear me! [*She closes her eyes tight and shivers her head.*]

MRS. FELL. Page eighteen did you say it was, Betty?

MRS. PAMPINELLI. Eighteen or nineteen, yes. It's somewhere right in there.

MRS. FELL. Oh, yes, here it is, I have it.

MRS. PAMPINELLI. [*Turning back to the people, and speaking with careful emphasis*] When you are going on and off the stage, be very careful of those little wooden strips that they have across the bottoms of the doors, and don't trip. [*Mrs. Ritter laughs self-consciously and Hossefrosse leans over and says something to her. Florence laughs, and turns and says something to Spindler, and Teddy and Twiller laugh and look toward Mrs. Ritter.*]

MRS. FELL. [*Looking out around Mrs. Pampinelli to see Mrs. Ritter*] Paula! [*Then she sits back, laughing, and says something to Ritter.*]

MRS. PAMPINELLI. I really think that was what made some of you so nervous at the Civic Club the last time. So, watch it, all of you, for they will probably have just the same thing down at Hutchy Kutchy.—There is perhaps nothing quite so disconcerting as to trip—as one comes on a stage. Going off—is not so bad; but—coming on, I have found that it requires a *tremendous* artist to rise above it. [*She starts down towards the table at the right, below the piano.*] So, watch it, all of you. Now, is everybody in his place? [*She stops below the table and picks up her note-book.*]

MRS. FELL. [*Handing Ritter the manuscript and getting up suddenly*] Oh, just one moment, Betty! [*She teeters across to the table at the right.*] I want to get my other glasses—they're right here in my bag. [*She picks up the bag and starts back to her place.*] I beg pardon, everybody, but I can't tell one letter from another without these glasses. [*This last sentence culminates in a flighty giggle, for no reason at all, and then she sits down, and heaves a deep sigh of amusement.*]

MRS. PAMPINELLI. [*Who has been looking at her steadily*] Now, is everybody ready? [*Mrs. Fell simply lifts her eyes and looks at her; then proceeds to get her glasses out of the bag.*] Use your voices, children, and try to do it tonight just as you are going to do it tomorrow night at Hutchy Kutchy. [*She moves a step or two nearer the middle of the room.*] Doctor Arlington is still in his office.

HOSSEFROSSE. Yes.

MRS. PAMPINELLI. Mr. Rush—

TWILLER. [*Coming in through the center-door*] Yes.

MRS. PAMPINELLI. Is just about to make his exit. [*He crosses above the piano and stands waiting at the right door. He's a bald-headed youth, between thirty and thirty-five, in dinner clothes, excessively well-groomed but utterly nondescript.*] And Mrs. Arlington is putting on the deadlatch. [*Florence straightens up.*] All ready, now? [*She holds up her hands for a second, then claps them once.*] All right. [*Twiller goes out through the right door and Mrs. Pampinelli moves over towards the right, watching Florence.*]

FLORENCE. [*Pretending to put on a deadlatch*] Deadlatch.

SPINDLER. [*Standing in rigid military fashion*] Click—click. [*Florence turns and starts across towards the middle of the room, passing between the piano and the table below it.*]

FLORENCE. [*Glancing toward the center-door*] You can come out now, Clyde, they've gone. [*She continues to the table at the left and stands resting one hand upon it.*]

HOSSEFROSSE. [*Bustling forward from the center-door, removing his hat as he comes*] Anybody here, David? [*Spindler whistles shrilly, takes a step forward and tries to attract Hossefrosse's attention, by holding up his right arm and flicking his fingers at him. Teddy laughs and turns to tell Twiller, who is just rejoining him from the right hallway, what has happened. Florence turns and looks at Hossefrosse, then at Mrs. Pampinelli, who is standing at the right of the table below the piano. Mrs. Ritter gets up and simply staggers laughing through the center-door and out to Teddy and Twiller.*]

FLORENCE. [*Speaking to Mrs. Pampinelli*] That isn't right, is it?

MRS. PAMPINELLI. [*Turning to Spindler at her right and holding up her hand*] Please don't whistle, Mr. Spindler! I can't stand whistling.

FLORENCE. I thought we were going to take the *last* scene first.

MRS. PAMPINELLI and MRS. FELL, together.

MRS. PAMPINELLI. [*Moving around in front of the table and going near to Hossefrosse*] We are taking the *last* scene *first*, Mr. Hossefrosse, that is the *first* scene.

MRS. FELL. [*Holding up her hand*] Wait a moment, wait one moment, just one moment, somebody's off the track! [*Twiller and Teddy laugh again and Hossefrosse turns and looks at them. Twiller shakes his head, flips his hand at him and walks away into the right hallway, as though deploring his stupidity. Ritter begins to laugh.*]

MRS. PAMPINELLI. I thought I had made that sufficiently clear.

MRS. PAMPINELLI, MRS. FELL, SPINDLER and TWILLER, together.

MRS. PAMPINELLI. We are taking the scene at the finish, Mr. Hossefrosse, between you and Miss McCrickett.

MRS. FELL. [*Rising*] That's the first scene, Huxley, and we are taking the last scene, between you and Florence, on page nineteen, right here, [*She indicates the place in the manuscript*].

SPINDLER. [*Addressing Teddy*] I hope he doesn't pull anything like that tomorrow night. [*He returns to his place below the window.*]

TWILLER. [*Coming back into view from the hallway*] Don't weaken, Huxley, you know what they say about a bad rehearsal.

MRS. PAMPINELLI. [*Topping them all*] Please, children, please!

MRS. FELL. Down at the bottom of the page. [*Mrs. Ritter comes through the center-door again and sits down on the left partition-seat.*]

MRS. PAMPINELLI. [*Speaking directly to Mrs. Fell*] Please—[*Mrs. Fell sits down again, slowly, Mrs. Pampinelli looking at her stonily.*] Let us have one director, if you please. [*She withdraws her eyes slowly, and Nelly darts a bitter look at her.*] Now, don't let us have everybody talking at once; it only confuses people, and wastes a lot of time. [*Hossefrosse stands bewildered in the middle of the room. Mrs. Pampinelli addresses him directly, speaking with measured emphasis.*] We are taking the *last* scene *first*, Mr. Hossefrosse: it is the scene at the finish, between you and Miss McCrickett, just before Paula comes on,—

HOSSEFROSSE. Oh, I beg your pardon!

MRS. PAMPINELLI. And *after* Mr. Rush has left the stage.

HOSSEFROSSE. I thought we were beginning right from the beginning.

MRS. PAMPINELLI. No, I'd like to run through the *last* scene *first*, if you don't mind; there are a few little things in it I'd like to correct.

HOSSEFROSSE. [*Turning and starting for the center-door*] This was the wrong entrance for that line, anyway.

MRS. PAMPINELLI. And you won't need your hat and cane in this scene.

HOSSEFROSSE. That's so, too.

TWILLER. [*Who is standing out just at the right of the center-door*] I'll take them, Hux.

HOSSEFROSSE. [*Handing him the hat, gloves and cane*] Thanks. [*Turning to Mrs. Ritter*] I'll get straightened out after while. [*Paula laughs.*]

MRS. PAMPINELLI. Now, Florence dear, will you go back?

FLORENCE. [*Crossing back again to the window*] Certainly.

MRS. PAMPINELLI. [*Crossing back to the right, in front of the table*] And take it right from Mr. Rush's exit.

FLORENCE. [*Looking round at Hossefrosse*] Ready?

HOSSEFROSSE. [*In the center-door*] Yes, I'm ready.

MRS. PAMPINELLI. [*To Florence*] Go on.

FLORENCE. [*Repeating her former business of putting on a deadlatch*] Deadlatch.

SPINDLER. [*Having again assumed his rigid military attitude*] Click—click. [*Florence turns and crosses again between the piano and the table.*]

FLORENCE. [*With a glance at the center-door*] You can come out now, Clyde, they've gone. [*She continues to her former position at the right of the little table at the left. Hossefrosse steps resolutely through the center-door, gives her a wicked look, glances toward the door at the right, then strides forward and plants himself directly opposite her, his head thrown back, his eyes ablaze, and his arms akimbo.*]

HOSSEFROSSE. Did you come here to make a scene!

FLORENCE. [*Languidly, and without turning*] Have I made one?

HOSSEFROSSE. [*Getting loud*] What are you doing here?

FLORENCE. [*Raising her hand to enjoin silence*] Sh-sh—[*He turns abruptly and looks toward the door at the right; then back to her again.*]

HOSSEFROSSE. I want an explanation of this!

FLORENCE. [*Turning to him, and rather casually*] So do I.

MRS. PAMPINELLI. [*Standing at the right of the table below the piano*] Oh, more imperious, Florence dear! [*Florence and Hossefrosse look at her.*] More of this. [*She lifts her shoulders, eyebrows and chin, to illustrate her idea of the general hauteur of the line.*] Much more.

FLORENCE. [*Vaguely*] Don't you think she would cry there? [*Mrs. Pampinelli looks at her steadily for a pause and thinks: then she rests her lead-pencil on the table and tilts her head a bit to one side.*]

MRS. PAMPINELLI. Do you want to cry there, dear?

FLORENCE. No, but I can if you want me to.

MRS. PAMPINELLI. No,—personally, I think she's speaking more in anger than in sorrow. You see, dear, you are impersonating a wronged wife. Now, you yourself, Florence darling, are an unmarried girl:—it is difficult for you to realize how excessively annoyed with her husband a married woman can become. I think I would take it with more *lift*. More of this, you know. [*She repeats her former illustration.*]

FLORENCE. [*Endeavoring to imitate the manner of delivery, and speaking in a deep, tragic tone*] So do I.

MRS. PAMPINELLI. Perfect.

HOSSEFROSSE. [*Turning to Mrs. Pampinelli*] Go on?

MRS. PAMPINELLI. Yes, go on.

HOSSEFROSSE. [*Clearing his throat and trying to summon his attack*] What is your reason for sneaking into my office at this hour?

FLORENCE. Is it necessary that your wife have a reason for coming to your office?

HOSSEFROSSE. You wanted to embarrass Mrs. Rush, that was it, wasn't it?

MRS. PAMPINELLI. [*Waving her hand toward them with an upward movement*] Tempo, children!

FLORENCE. I wanted to meet my rival.

HOSSEFROSSE. You could have met Mrs. Rush under more candid circumstances.

MRS. PAMPINELLI. [*Moving around towards them, in front of the table*] Tempo, children!

FLORENCE. The present ones suited my purposes better.

HOSSEFROSSE. [*Turning away impatiently*] Naturally!—You wanted a scene! [*He starts over to the right, but Mrs. Pampinelli is standing right in his way, so he stops short, but maintains the physical tautness of his character. Florence, too, has turned away, to the left, and is moving across in front of the table towards the arm-chair.*]

MRS. PAMPINELLI. [*Oblivious of Hossefrosse, and still making her upward waving gesture over his shoulder*] Tempo, Florence! [*Suddenly becoming conscious that she is obstructing Hossefrosse's cross, and stepping below him*] I beg your pardon.

HOSSEFROSSE. [*Bowing stiffly*] Not at all. [*He continues over to the right and stops, right in front of Spindler, and they stand looking into each other's eyes; while Mrs. Pampinelli comes up at the left of the table to the piano.*]

FLORENCE. [*Sitting down in the arm-chair*] I think if I were a scenic woman I've had ample opportunity during the last fifteen minutes to indulge myself.

HOSSEFROSSE. [*Still looking into Spindler's eyes*] You did I think;—

MRS. PAMPINELLI. [*Beckoning to Spindler*] Mr. Spindler.

HOSSEFROSSE. I had the pleasure of hearing you.

FLORENCE. Was it a pleasure, Clyde?

MRS. PAMPINELLI and HOSSEFROSSE, together.

> MRS. PAMPINELLI. [*Still beckoning to Spindler*] Mr. Spindler!
>
> HOSSEFROSSE. [*Whirling around and glaring at Florence*] It appears to amuse you! [*Spindler steps below Hossefrosse and passes up in front of him to Mrs. Pampinelli, who whispers something to him.*]

FLORENCE. [*Unfastening her neckpiece*] I have an inopportune sense of humor.

HOSSEFROSSE. You should be able to appreciate the situation, you created it!

FLORENCE. [*Looking over at him*] I didn't create her husband.

HOSSEFROSSE. [*Making a little gesture of annoyance*] I'm afraid I'm stuck! [*He tries hard to think, and Mrs. Pampinelli makes a gesture toward Mrs. Fell to give him the line, but Nelly is occupied in telling Ritter a story.*] But, don't tell me! [*He feels for the line again, and Mrs. Pampinelli tries to attract Nelly's attention.*] I guess I'm gone. [*Suddenly Nelly bursts into a fit of laughing, having made the point of the story.*]

MRS. PAMPINELLI. What is the line, Nelly? [*Ritter nudges her.*]

MRS. FELL. [*Stopping suddenly in her laughter and hitting him with her fan*] Stop that!

RITTER. Get on your job, you're holding up the show. [*Nelly looks excitedly toward Mrs. Pampinelli.*]

MRS. PAMPINELLI. What is the line, Nelly, please.

MRS. FELL. What! Oh, I beg your pardon, is somebody stuck?

MRS. PAMPINELLI. Mr. Hossefrosse.

HOSSEFROSSE. Got another mind-blank.

MRS. FELL. Oh, well, now, just wait one minute, please, till I see where I'm at. [*She searches frantically through the manuscript.*] Oh, yes, here it is! [*Ritter indicates a place on the page. She pushes his arm out of the way.*] I didn't create her husband. [*Teddy and Twiller laugh.*]

MRS. PAMPINELLI, FLORENCE and HOSSEFROSSE, together.

> MRS. PAMPINELLI. No, dear, we've just passed that.
>
> FLORENCE. I've already said that, Nelly.
>
> HOSSEFROSSE. It's the next line.

MRS. FELL. [*Vaguely, and looking through her lorgnon and spectacles at the manuscript*] Oh, have we passed that!

MRS. PAMPINELLI. The next line after the one you just read.

MRS. FELL. Oh, I see now where we are! The next line after that is, "You've all been listening to a lot of damned, cheap gossip."

MRS. PAMPINELLI and HOSSEFROSSE, together.

> MRS. PAMPINELLI. That's it.
>
> HOSSEFROSSE. [*To Mrs. Pampinelli*] That certainly is my Jonah line.

MRS. PAMPINELLI. You've all been list—[*Spindler goes around to the right and sits on the piano-stool, looking near-sightedly at the music.*]

HOSSEFROSSE. [*Turning to Florence, and assuming his character again*] You've all been listening to a lot of damned, cheap gossip! [*He starts to cross towards the left, passing between the piano and the table, but Mrs. Pampinelli is right in his way again, so he is obliged to stop short and wait.*]

FLORENCE. Which should show you that people are talking. [*Mrs. Pampinelli turns to see why Hossefrosse is not picking up his line.*]

MRS. PAMPINELLI. [*Stepping out of his way*] I beg your pardon. [*She circles down at the left of the table again.*]

HOSSEFROSSE. [*Continuing over towards the mantelpiece*] My fault. One or two old women, perhaps.

FLORENCE. Will it confine itself to those?

HOSSEFROSSE. [*Turning at the mantelpiece and coming back to the middle of the room*] Well, I can't control that.

FLORENCE. Have you tried?

HOSSEFROSSE. [*Whirling upon her, and literally shouting*] No!

MRS. PAMPINELLI. [*Standing at the right of the table below the piano*] Excellent.

HOSSEFROSSE. [*Turning and bowing briefly to her*] Thank you very much. [*Resuming the scene with Florence*] And I don't intend to. People will always talk; it may as well be at my expense as anybody else's.

MRS. PAMPINELLI. [*Leaning towards him across the table, and speaking with poisonous sweetness*] Anybody's *else*, dear.

HOSSEFROSSE. Beg pardon?

MRS. PAMPINELLI. Would you say anybody's else; it sounds better.

HOSSEFROSSE. [*Turning back again to Florence*] It may as well be at my expense as anybody else's. [*Mr. Spindler's elbow slips off the piano onto the keyboard, striking a perfectly villainous chord, and causing everybody to turn and look in that direction.*]

MRS. PAMPINELLI. Mr. Spindler, please.

SPINDLER. [*Adjusting his goggles, which have been slightly dislodged by the incident*] I'm sorry. [*Mrs. Pampinelli turns back to Hossefrosse.*] Never mind, Mr. Hossefrosse, it will come.

FLORENCE. Your position can't afford it.

HOSSEFROSSE. [*Taking a step towards the right*] I've given them nothing to talk about.

FLORENCE. No? [*He stops abruptly and turns and looks at her.*]

HOSSEFROSSE. What? [*He takes a couple of steps towards her.*]

FLORENCE. [*Rising*] Please, Clyde!—[*She crosses in front of the table at the left and goes towards him. Mrs. Ritter gets up from the partition-seat and comes down to the table at the right, below the piano.*] You're not talking to your office-boy—[*Mrs. Ritter picks up the little chair from the left of the table and starts back again towards the center-door.*] Let us get to the point.

HOSSEFROSSE. Very well.

MRS. RITTER and HOSSEFROSSE, together.

> MRS. RITTER.—Excuse me, Florence. [*Florence bows and smiles.*] And you, too, Mr. Hossefrosse.

HOSSEFROSSE. What brought you here tonight? [*He turns to see the cause of the movement behind him.*] Don't mention it. [*Mrs. Ritter places the chair in front of the partition where she has been sitting, then crosses to the piano and gets her sewing-basket, returning with it to the chair and sitting down to sew.*]

FLORENCE. Not to quarrel with you, for one thing.

HOSSEFROSSE. You wanted to embarrass Mrs. Rush, that was it, wasn't it?

FLORENCE. Not at all,—you misunderstood me; I said, "I wanted to *meet* Mrs. Rush." [*Teddy comes in through the center-door from the right hallway and sits down on the partition-seat at the right. Teddy is a frail little wisp of a youth around twenty, in dinner clothes. He has big eyes and good teeth, and laughs on the slightest provocation. His forehead is defectively high, and his thin hair is plastered back and brilliantined. His type is always to be found draped upon the banisters or across the pianos in the houses of the rich,—a kind of social annoyance, created by wealthy connections and the usual lack of available men.*]

HOSSEFROSSE. What did you want to meet her for? [*Twiller steps through the center-door from the right hallway and whispers something to Mrs. Ritter. She answers him, and he steps out into the hallway and fills himself out a glass of claret from the bowl, then goes up and sits on the landing of the stairway and watches the rehearsal.*]

FLORENCE. Why, I thought that we three might—reason together, [*He holds her eye for a second, then turns away, and reaches in his various pockets for his cigarettes.*] concerning our respective futures.

HOSSEFROSSE. [*In a lowered tone, to Mrs. Pampinelli*] Forgot my cigarettes.

MRS. PAMPINELLI. Never mind, I only want lines. Go on, Florence. [*Hossefrosse takes an imaginary cigarette from an imaginary case, replaces the case, taps the cigarette on the back of his hand, puts it in his mouth, strikes an imaginary match on his shoe, and lights the cigarette.*]

FLORENCE. I've deferred the discussion for a long time, but it may as well be today as tomorrow.

HOSSEFROSSE. Your plan didn't work out very well, did it?

FLORENCE. Oh, yes, very well indeed; although hardly as I had anticipated; thanks to *her* husband and *your* lies. [*He blows out the imaginary match and tosses it onto the floor at the right; then snaps his head around and glares at Florence. Mrs. Pampinelli glances down onto the floor, as though to assure herself that Mr. Hossefrosse hasn't really thrown a lighted match onto the carpet.*] You've evidently told this boy here that Mrs. Rush is your wife.

HOSSEFROSSE. I've told him nothing of the kind! [*He starts to cross again to the right, but Mrs. Pampinelli is again right in his pathway, standing in front of the table below the piano.*]

MRS. PAMPINELLI. [*Stepping below him, and going a step or two nearer Florence*] I beg your pardon.

HOSSEFROSSE. I beg your pardon. [*He continues over to the table below the window at the right and stands there, pretending to smoke.*]

FLORENCE. Then, you've allowed him to think so.

HOSSEFROSSE. [*Looking straight ahead*] That's business.

FLORENCE. Perhaps it is. It has at least allowed you to be present at the passing of Mrs. Rush. [*She turns and goes towards the back. Mrs. Ritter calls her to her and they start discussing the hang of Florence's skirt.*]

HOSSEFROSSE. [*Whirling around*] You are deliberately misinterpreting this situation! [*He starts to move across towards her, passing between the piano and table.*] Yes you are! It's perfectly ridiculous that a physician cannot take a woman patient without being subjected to the whisperings of a lot of vulgar scandal-mongers! [*Nelly Fell goes into violent laughter at something Ritter has just finished telling her. Florence and Mrs. Ritter continue their discussion of the dress, and Mrs. Pampinelli tries by dint of gesturing to attract Florence's attention.*]

MRS. PAMPINELLI. Florence dear, please.

FLORENCE. [*Turning suddenly, and continuing her lines*] Oh, I beg your pardon! [*She moves slowly towards the mantelpiece.*] This is not a romantic age, Clyde.

HOSSEFROSSE. Mrs. Rush is a patient of mine!

FLORENCE. [*Moving down at the left towards Ritter and Mrs. Fell*] She may have been originally. [*Mrs. Fell bursts out afresh over something else that Ritter whispers.*]

MRS. PAMPINELLI. [*Flicking her finger at Nelly*] Sh-sh-Nelly.

MRS. FELL. [*To Florence, who is standing looking at her*] I beg your pardon.

HOSSEFROSSE. [*Standing in the middle of the room*] She is *now*!

FLORENCE. [*Resting one hand on the arm-chair*] I'm not disputing it. [*He turns away, and stands at the left of the table below the piano.*] But she must have a very persistent malady—

MRS. FELL. Just one minute, Flossie—one minute—

FLORENCE. That hasn't responded to a treatment of more than six years—

MRS. FELL. Flossie, Flossie, Flossie! [*Florence stops and looks at her.*] Just a minute. [*She looks sharply at her manuscript.*]

MRS. PAMPINELLI. What is the matter, Nelly?

MRS. FELL. Oh, I beg your pardon, I thought she'd omitted a line. [*To Florence*] I beg your pardon.

MRS. PAMPINELLI. Go on, Florence. [*Ritter says something to Nelly and she hits him with the manuscript.*]

FLORENCE. Not to speak of the innumerable changes of air that she's enjoyed—[*Mrs. Pampinelli, standing over at the right below the piano, takes quite a little coughing spell, and Mrs. Ritter promptly gets up and goes to the punch-bowl to fill her out a glass of punch.*] at your expense; and under your personal escort. [*Hossefrosse looks over at her. She raises her hand understandingly, and starts slowly across in front of the table towards him.*] I have the day and date of the majority of them. So, you see, your chivalry is a bit trying, under the circumstances. [*He looks straight ahead and tries to look sullen and defeated.*]

MRS. RITTER. [*Up in the center-door, holding aloft a glass of punch*] Betty!

FLORENCE. But, I haven't come here to reproach you, or to plead for your return. Not at all. I think you *love* this woman.

MRS. RITTER. [*Coming a little further forward*] Betty! [*Mrs. Pampinelli has another coughing spell.*]

FLORENCE. And in that case, I want to offer you your freedom—

MRS. PAMPINELLI. Careful, now, children. [*Mrs. Ritter comes forward to the table at the left and tries to attract Mrs. Pampinelli's attention to the glass of punch.*]

FLORENCE. If you want it.

MRS. PAMPINELLI. [*Holding up her forefinger*] One, two, three.

HOSSEFROSSE. [*Snapping his head around and shouting at Florence*] Well, I don't want it!

MRS. PAMPINELLI. Good!

HOSSEFROSSE. And I see absolutely no occasion for any such talk. [*Mrs. Fell drops her bag and reaches for it.*]

FLORENCE. You are probably more broad-minded than I. [*Nelly Fell utters a piercing little shriek, having almost fallen off the chair in reaching to pick up her bag. Everyone turns and looks, and Teddy laughs, as usual.*]

MRS. PAMPINELLI. What's the matter, Nelly?

MRS. FELL. [*Straightening up, with Ritter's assistance, and laughing*] I nearly fell off the chair. [*Mrs. Ritter laughs and returns to the center-door and stands.*]

MRS. PAMPINELLI. Go on, Florence.

FLORENCE. And, really, I don't think your freedom would be a very good thing for you. You have a form of respectability that requires a certain anchorage in the conventions. But unless you can reconcile yourself in the future to a more literal observance of those conventions, I shall be obliged to insist that you *take* your freedom.

MRS. PAMPINELLI. Look at her, Mr. Hossefrosse.

HOSSEFROSSE. Beg pardon?

MRS. PAMPINELLI. [*With a touch of impatience*] Look at her! [*She begins to cough again.*]

HOSSEFROSSE. Oh, yes, yes! [*He turns and glares at Florence, who is standing just a couple of feet away from him.*]

MRS. RITTER. [*Holding the glass of punch aloft again*] Betty!

FLORENCE. I have a couple of growing boys,—[*Mrs. Pampinelli passes right up between Florence and Hossefrosse to Mrs. Ritter, and takes the glass of claret.*] who are beginning to ask me questions which I find too difficult to answer: and I will neither lie to them—nor allow them to pity me.

HOSSEFROSSE. What do you want me to do?

MRS. PAMPINELLI. [*Handing the claret-glass back to Paula, who goes to the bowl and refills it, and the note-book and pencil to Teddy*] Just a moment. [*She turns and comes forward in the middle of the room. Florence turns and moves over to the table at the left, and Hossefrosse remains standing at the table at the right.*] Just one moment. Listen, Florence dear. [*She uses her handkerchief, then stuffs it into the bosom of her dress.*] I want you, if you can, to make just a little bit more of that last line. Within the limits of the characterization, of course; but if you can *feel* it, I'd like you to give me just the barest suggestion of a tear. Not too much; but just enough to show that,—under all her courage—and her threatening, she is still a woman—and a Mother. You see what I mean, dear?

FLORENCE. More emotion.

MRS. PAMPINELLI. In that last line. You are doing splendidly, darling, [*Turning to Hossefrosse*] both of you; [*He acknowledges his excellence with a short bow.*] but I have always *felt* that that last line—was really the *big* moment—of the play. It seems to me—[*She toys with her necklace, narrows her eyes and looks away off.*] that it is there—that she makes her big plea, for her boys, for her home,—for every woman's home. And even though that plea *is* made in the form of a threat,—somehow or other—I seem to hear her saying, sub-vocally, of course, "In God's *name, don't* make it necessary for me to do this thing!" [*She concludes this speech rather dramatically, her arms outstretched. Mr. Spindler, at this point, engaged in a too curious examination of the keyboard, accidentally* touches D flat above High C. *Everybody turns and looks at him, but his consciousness of guilt does not permit of his meeting their eyes, so he remains bent over the keyboard in precisely the attitude he was in when he struck the note.*]

MRS. FELL. Oh, go away from that piano, Mr. Spindler! [*Mrs. Ritter comes forward at the left with a dish of cakes and a glass of claret.*]

MRS. PAMPINELLI. [*Withdrawing her eyes witheringly from Spindler and turning back to Florence*] Do you see what I mean, dear?

FLORENCE. I think I do. Do you want me to go back?

MRS. PAMPINELLI. No, that's quite all right. We'll take it right from Mr. Hossefrosse's line, [*She turns toward Hossefrosse. And Mrs. Ritter takes advantage of the circumstance to offer Florence a cake; which, of course, is declined with thanks. Then she turns to Mrs. Pampinelli and waits till the lady has finished directing Hossefrosse.*] "What do you want me to do?" [*Mrs. P. turns back, to be confronted with the cakes and claret; and she takes both. Then she and Paula move back towards the center-door.*]

HOSSEFROSSE. [*Clearing his throat*] What do you want me to do? [*Paula gives a shriek of laughter, at something Mrs. Pampinelli whispers to her. Then Paula goes out through the center-door and offers Twiller, who is still sitting half-way up the stairs, some cake, which he accepts, and then Teddy, who declines, and finally, after taking another one herself, sets the plate down on the hallway table and resumes her chair up at the left; while Mrs. Pampinelli, cake and claret in hand, wanders forward at the right, passing over between the piano and the table below it.*]

FLORENCE. I've already told you.

HOSSEFROSSE. Then, I suppose I'm simply to decline all women patients in the future, [*She makes a little sound of amusement.*] or else submit them for general approval. [*He now presses the imaginary fire out of the cigarette on the imaginary tray on the table.*]

FLORENCE. Stick to your guns, Clyde.

HOSSEFROSSE. That's the only thing I see to do. [*Mrs. Pampinelli stands over at the right watching the scene, and eating and drinking.*]

FLORENCE. Your tenacity is commendable, but it's a lost cause. [*Looking at him steadily*] I appreciate your embarrassment—

HOSSEFROSSE. [*Turning to her, thrusting his hands into his coat-pockets, tilting his chin, and looking at her with an absurdly perky expression*] I'm not embarrassed.

FLORENCE. Desolation, then.

HOSSEFROSSE. [*Snapping his fingers at her*] Ha! [*He swings rather jauntily across and up towards the mantelpiece.*]

MRS. PAMPINELLI. More nonchalance in the cross, Mr. Hossefrosse.

HOSSEFROSSE. [*Turning to her suddenly*] Me?

MRS. PAMPINELLI. More savoir faire, as we say in French. [*She illustrates the idea with a kind of floating gesture of the hand.*]

HOSSEFROSSE. I see. [*He continues over to the left and down towards Ritter and Mrs. Fell, endeavoring to execute Mrs. Pampinelli's idea by raising his shoulders, stiffening his arms, throwing his head back and swinging his legs, as he walks. Nelly Fell is whispering something to Ritter behind her fan, so that, when Hossefrosse reaches them, he is obliged to touch Ritter on the shoulder and suggest with a nod and a smile that the exigencies of the play require that he shall sit where Ritter is sitting. So Ritter jumps up and tiptoes across in front of the table and up to the piano, where he stands leaning—and watching— particularly Mrs. Pampinelli.*]

FLORENCE. [*Moving to the table below the piano*] But, I shall be magnanimous; having loved and lost myself. So that, really, it may not be nearly so difficult as you imagine.

HOSSEFROSSE. [*Sitting on the chair vacated by Ritter*] Well, I can't say that I relish the prospect, with any such misunderstanding as this between us.

FLORENCE. [*Crossing to the table at the left*] It's the portion of half the world, Clyde. [*Twiller gets up from the stairs and comes down into the right hallway, where he stands watching.*]

HOSSEFROSSE. [*Trying to look sullen, by resting one elbow on his knee and hunching his shoulders*] It certainly isn't a very inviting one. [*Nelly Fell starts to whisper something in his ear.*]

FLORENCE. But it has its compensations. [*Mrs. Pampinelli, having finished her cake and claret, sets the empty glass down on the table below the piano and uses her handkerchief.*] You'll have your memories, and I shall have the wisdom of disillusionment;—[*The telephone-bell rings, up in the left hallway. Mrs. Ritter jumps up, places her sewing-basket on the chair, and, touching her hair, comes forward quickly at the right to the table below the piano.*] as well as the consciousness of lots of company.

MRS. RITTER. [*Speaking directly to Mrs. Pampinelli*] Is that my cue? [*Florence stops and turns and looks at her.*]

MRS. PAMPINELLI. Which cue, dear?

MRS. RITTER. [*Taking a step towards Florence, and with a little questioning, bewildered gesture*] The telephone is my cue, isn't it?

MRS. PAMPINELLI. [*With a touch of impatience*] No, darling, you're not on in this scene at all. Go on, Florence. [*Mrs. Ritter puts her hand to her cheek and looks from one to the other in puzzled embarrassment.*]

FLORENCE. [*Turning and resuming her lines to Hossefrosse, who, by this time, is deep in conversation with Mrs. Fell*] For there are a million women exactly like me. [*Mrs. Ritter bursts out laughing. So does Teddy. Twiller reaches over the partition and flips Teddy on the head with his handkerchief. Jenny appears in the left hallway to answer the telephone.*]

MRS. RITTER and FLORENCE, together.

> MRS. RITTER. [*Turning to Mrs. Pampinelli*] Oh, I beg your pardon! [*She leans across the table explaining to Mrs. Pampinelli, who tries politely to silence her by suggestion that the scene is in progress.*] I thought that was my cue.
>
> FLORENCE—Secondary women. [*She moves around above the table and stands just above Hossefrosse.*] So don't look so tragic; you haven't lost anything but a lot of time;

JENNY. [*At the telephone*] Hello?

MRS. RITTER, FLORENCE and MRS. FELL, together.

> MRS. RITTER.—I was thinking of something else, you know, and when I heard the telephone, I thought it was for me.
>
> FLORENCE.—And that's always lost when it's spent on things that are insusceptible of conclusion.
>
> MRS. FELL. [*Bursting into a perfect shriek of laughter at something Hossefrosse has just finished telling her, and pushing him away from her*] Huxley Hossefrosse, you are perfectly dreadful! [*He laughs, too, and attempts to tell her something else, but she turns away and waves him aside.*] No, No, No.

MRS. PAMPINELLI. No dear, that is your own telephone.

JENNY. [*At the telephone still*] Just a minute. [*Mrs. Ritter turns towards the back of the room.*]

MRS. RITTER. Oh, so it is! [*Directly to Ritter*] I knew I had one telephone cue. [*She goes laughing through the center-door and on out into the right hallway.*]

JENNY. [*Trying to attract Ritter's attention*] MR. RITTER! [*But Ritter is absorbed in watching Hossefrosse. Florence stands waiting for Hossefrosse and Nelly to stop laughing, but as it doesn't look as though they will ever stop, she gives Hossefrosse a little dig in the shoulder with her finger. He straightens up abruptly.*]

FLORENCE. [*Prompting him*] I've lost her.

JENNY. Mr. Ritter!

HOSSEFROSSE. I've lost her.

FLORENCE. That was inevitable in your case, Clyde; you have a conventional soul. [*Jenny asks Teddy in pantomime to attract Ritter's attention.*]

HOSSEFROSSE. [*In a tone intended to express abysmal despair*] I've lost you. [*Ritter bursts out laughing. Teddy reaches out and indicates that he is wanted on the telephone. Jenny holds the telephone up, and he steps quickly out into the hallway to take it from her.*]

FLORENCE. That was incidental, eh?

HOSSEFROSSE. But, it seems to me there should be some other way.

FLORENCE. [*Moving to the right, above the table*] There is, my dear boy,—for lots of people——

RITTER. [*at the telephone*] Hello? [*Jenny goes out.*]

FLORENCE. But not for you.

RITTER. Yes.

FLORENCE. You're too respectable—Physically, I mean. [*She laughs a little, and stands above the table looking at him.*]

RITTER. Well, wait a minute, I'll talk to you upstairs. [*He sets the telephone down and starts towards the right to go upstairs. As he passes the center-door he speaks to Teddy, who is still sitting just inside the center-door on the right partition-seat.*] Hang that up when I get on, will you, Teddy? [*Teddy jumps up and goes out to the telephone, and holds it, waiting till Ritter gets on the extension upstairs.*]

FLORENCE. And Mrs. Rush has what it appears to me to be a rather— primitive husband—[*Hossefrosse gives her a narrow look.*] and you have a very modern wife. So be wise, Clyde; you know what usually happens to him who "loves the danger." [*There is a loud knock at the right door. Hossefrosse jumps to his feet and stands looking fearfully toward it. Florence assumes all the dignity at her command, drawing herself up, placing her right hand upon her throat, her left on her hip, and waiting,—the proud but outraged wife. Mrs. Pampinelli holds up both hands and looks in the direction of the door, to impress everybody with the dramatic value of the situation. Teddy hangs up the receiver and stands watching her. Nelly Fell straightens up briskly and sits watching the door, in expectant attention. Then Mrs. Pampinelli makes a gesture to Florence to go on with her lines.*] Go into your office, I'll talk to this woman. [*Hossefrosse drops his head and shoulders and slinks across in front of the table, a beaten man. He continues up to the center-door and out, into the right hallway. The knock is repeated at the right door. Mrs. Pampinelli motions to Teddy that that is his cue to open the door. He comes through the center-door and crosses above the piano to the right door,*

Mrs. Pampinelli at the same time moving over to the arm-chair at the right and enshrining herself. Teddy opens the door; and Mrs. Ritter swishes in self-consciously. Nelly Fell and Mr. Twiller give a little ripple of applause, but Mrs. Pampinelli holds one finger up toward Nelly and shushes her. Mrs. Ritter is wearing a rather bizarre-looking hat, set at something of a challenging angle, and as she comes forward at the right of the piano, she bursts into a self-conscious giggle. But Mrs. Pampinelli reproves her with a look. So she controls herself and crosses below the piano, Teddy, simultaneously, crossing above the piano. She stops at the corner of the piano and rests her left hand upon it. Then she places her right hand upon her hip, and, tilting her head back, looks at Teddy, who has stopped directly above her. Ritter appears on the stairway, and moves down a step or two, watching his wife, narrowly.]

MRS. RITTER. [*Flipping her left hand at Teddy, in an attempt to give a fly impression*] Hello, kid.

TEDDY. Hello, Mrs. Arlington. [*Mrs. Ritter swishes down towards the left, shaking her head from side to side and holding her arms akimbo. She turns around to her left, gives Florence a look, supposed to be a very contemptuous look, and stands in the middle of the room again, facing Teddy.*]

MRS. RITTER. [*Speaking directly to Teddy*] Is my sweetie in? [*Ritter moves slowly down to the landing of the stairs, watching his wife as though she were some baffling phenomenon.*]

TEDDY. No, mam, he ain't.

MRS. RITTER. [*Drawing her shoulders up, and speaking in a high unnatural key*] What!

TEDDY. He went about six o'clock.

MRS. RITTER. Why, I had an appointment with *him*!

TEDDY. He might be back, maybe.

MRS. RITTER. But, I can't wait unless I'm *certain* that he's coming back.

TEDDY. He was expecting you.

MRS. RITTER. [*Still shaking her head and trying generally to appear bold*] Yes, I know he was. [*Turning to the table at the left, back of which Florence is standing*] I suppose I'd better leave a note for him. [*She indicates the table with a waving gesture of her left hand.*]

TEDDY. You'll find that green one is the best pen.

MRS. RITTER. [*Stepping to the table*] Thanks. [*She looks at Florence, who gives her a withering look over her right shoulder and turns away to the mantelpiece at the left. Then Mrs. Ritter gives her idea of a scornful laugh.*] Ha! Ha! Ha!

RITTER. [*Sweeping his hand across his brow, groaning, and falling down the stairs, into the right hallway*] Oh my God!

MRS. PAMPINELLI. [*Seeing him fall, and jumping up*] Oh, my dear! [*Everybody turns.*]

TWILLER. [*Trying to catch him*] Hold it! [*Spindler rushes past Mrs. Pampinelli and out the center-door into the right hallway. Teddy jumps into a kneeling position on the right partition-seat and looks over the partition. Florence and Mrs. Fell rush up to the center-door and try to see what's going on, Nelly dodging from one side of Florence to the other, and peering through her lorgnon.*] Are you hurt, old man?

HOSSEFROSSE. [*Handing his cane and gloves to Spindler*] Hold those, please. [*Spindler takes them, and Hossefrosse prepares to assist Twiller to lift Ritter from the floor.*]

TWILLER. Get some water, somebody! [*Spindler rushes out the left hallway. Mrs. Pampinelli sweeps up from below the table at the right to the center-door.*]

MRS. RITTER. [*Bewildered, in the middle of the room, as Mrs. Pampinelli passes her*] What is it, Betty?

MRS. PAMPINELLI. Now, don't get excited, Paula. [*Mrs. Ritter steps frantically across to the piano and turns, leaning against it, looking wide-eyed at Nelly Fell.*]

HOSSEFROSSE. Lift up his head.

MRS. PAMPINELLI. [*Looking eagerly out into the right hallway*] Is he hurt, boys?

TWILLER. I want to get him under the arms. [*They lift Ritter onto a bench in the hallway. Nelly Fell turns away from the center-door with an exclamation of distress.*]

HOSSEFROSSE. We'd better lay him right here.

MRS. RITTER. Is it Fred, Nelly?

MRS. FELL. I don't know, dear.

MRS. PAMPINELLI and MRS. FELL, together.

> MRS. PAMPINELLI. [*Addressing Hossefrosse and Twiller*] You can lay him right here, boys, I think it'll be as good as any.
>
> MRS. FELL. What is it, Florence, did Mr. Ritter fall downstairs?

FLORENCE. I think so.

MRS. FELL. [*Covering her eyes and swaying*] Oh, dear child, don't! [*Florence puts her arm around her and guides her towards the arm-chair at the left.*]

MRS. PAMPINELLI. Give me one of those pillows, Teddy. [*He hands her a pillow from the partition-seat where he's kneeling.*]

MRS. FELL. [*Sinking into the arm-chair at the left*] Betty, I think I'm going to faint!

MRS. PAMPINELLI. [*Turning to her*] Sit down, dear, I'll get you some water. [*Calling and beckoning out into the left hallway*] Jenny dear! come here, please!

HOSSEFROSSE. [*Rushing across from the right to the left hallway*] I think I'd better call Dr. Wentworth. [*He snatches up the telephone and works the hook violently.*]

MRS. PAMPINELLI. Yes, I would. [*She turns around to her left and stands looking questioningly at Mrs. Ritter.*] Go on with your lines, Paula.

MRS. RITTER. Well, is he *dead*, Betty?

MRS. PAMPINELLI. [*With a definite little gesture of her right hand*] Never mind! [*The curtain commences to descend, and she sweeps forward.*] We will go right on from where Mr. Ritter fell downstairs.

THE CURTAIN IS DOWN

AS IT RISES AGAIN FOR THE PICTURE

HOSSEFROSSE. [*At the telephone*] Landsdowne 8, please,—right away! [*Spindler rushes in from the left hallway carrying a glass of water, and followed immediately by Jenny. Twiller is ministering to Ritter. Mrs. Pampinelli is standing in the middle of the room, facing the center-door, and holding up both her hands, as a signal to the various artists that the rehearsal is about to be resumed; so they quickly step to the various positions in which they respectively were when Mr. Ritter fell.*]

MRS. RITTER. [*Addressing Teddy*] Yes, I know he was. I s'pose I'd better leave a note for him.

END OF THE ACT

THE TORCH-BEARERS—ACT II.

NOTE:

The setting for this act consists simply of three wings set in the middle of the stage about four feet from the footlights, and parallel to the footlights, the wing in the middle, a plain one, and the one on either side of it, a door-wing. These doors open toward the footlights, and the one on the right is hinged to the right, and the one on the left, to the left. From these door-wings, regular plain wings oblique off to the back wall; and the whole thing is lashed and stage-screwed after the fashion of regulation stage-setting. As the doors in the back flat open, there can be had a glimpse of footlights, and just beyond them, a neutral drop, in grayish black, to represent an auditorium. Between the back flat and the stage footlights, (as distinguished from the regular footlights) the miniature stage is set to represent the interior of a doctor's waiting-room. Through the door at the right can be seen a desk and revolving chair, and a couple of plain chairs against the wall; and through the left door, a table, littered with magazines, a cabinet, a revolving bookcase and two more chairs. There is a bright rug on the floor. Between the back flat and the regular footlights, over toward the left, there is a stage-screw sticking right up out of the floor; and between the two doors there is a plain chair with its back against the flat. Over the door on the right, there is a row of six electric bulbs with a cord and button depending from it; and further right, half-way back, there is a wood-wing, set as though it were the exterior backing for a window in the miniature set. Over at the left, away back, fastened about head-high against the back wall, there is a small switchboard-arrangement. Just below this there is an old chair, without a back, with a newspaper lying upon it.

THE TORCH-BEARERS—ACT II.

A waltz is being played somewhere off at the right. Florence and Mrs. Ritter are standing in the middle of the stage, facing the flats, talking. Florence is wearing a fawn-colored, one-piece coat-dress, buttoned high at the throat, military fashion, and a toque made of wine-colored velvet leaves. She wears fawn-colored slippers and stockings, and carries a fitch muff. Mrs. Ritter is wearing a very rich-looking coat-suit in blue serge, trimmed at the collar and cuffs with white monkey-fur. Her hat is dark-blue felt, quite large, with a bird of paradise set at a decidedly rakish tilt. Her slippers and stockings are black, and she carries an umbrella. Over at the extreme left, and forward, Mrs. Fell is hearing Mr. Twiller read his lines from the manuscript. Mrs. Fell is gowned in a brilliant creation of silver-cloth trimmed with sea-green satin. There are numerous strings of crystal beads hanging in the front from the waist to the bottom of the skirt, and she has a spreading poinsetta in scarlet velvet fastened at her waist. There is a long, fish-tail train to the gown, lined with the green satin, and she has a heavy rope of pearls and sea-green beads around her neck, from which her lorgnon depends. There are diamonds in her hair, diamonds galore upon her arms and hands, and she's wearing her diamond dog-collar. Her slippers and stockings are of pale green. Mr. Twiller has on a double-breasted blue-serge suit, a black derby, black shoes and fawn-colored spats, and a perfectly villainous-looking black mustache, absurdly large, and obviously artificial. He stands leaning upon a cane, reciting his lines to Mrs. Fell. Mr. Spindler, in a dinner-suit, is trying desperately to unfasten the stage-screw from the floor at the left, while Mr. Hossefrosse, wearing a light business-suit, a light, soft hat, tan shoes and spats, and carrying a cane and gloves, is pacing back and forth between the left door and the extreme left, reciting his lines to himself. He is atrociously made up, with the carmine smeared heavily on his cheek-bones. The stage manager, in a tan jumper and army shirt, dirty white running-pumps, a battered old cap adorned with many tobacco-tags, and carrying a hammer, wanders on from the right and crosses the stage, passing below Florence and Mrs. Ritter, who turn and look at him curiously, and continues on up at the left to the switch-board, where he picks up the newspaper from the broken chair, and, after lighting his pipe, sits down to read. He is apparently disgusted with the world and utterly oblivious of his surroundings. The waltz-music stops, and Mr. Hossefrosse comes to a halt in his pacing, right outside the left door. It is instantly flung open, knocking him toward the left, and disarranging his hat, and Mrs. Pampinelli sweeps out—in a princess-gown of ruby-colored velvet, with a long train, and heavily trimmed about the upper part of the bodice with ornaments of ruby-colored beads. Her shoulders and arms are bare, and she has a small string of rubies about her throat;—a bracelet and several rings of rubies; as well as a high Spanish comb studded with rubies. Her slippers are of black velvet. Mrs. Ritter gives a little cry as Mr. Hossefrosse is struck by the door.

MRS. PAMPINELLI. [*Holding the door ajar*] Oh, did I hit you, Mr. Hossefrosse! I'm so sorry.

HOSSEFROSSE. [*Settling his hat*] That's all right.

MRS. PAMPINELLI. [*To the ladies*] The setting looks splendid, girls! [*Crossing quickly below Hossefrosse towards the left*] Will you come here for a moment, Mr. Spindler?

MRS. RITTER. [*Turning away to the right*] I don't want to see it till I go on.

FLORENCE. [*As Hossefrosse comes towards her*] You'd better keep away from that door, Mr. Hossefrosse. [*She and Mrs. Ritter laugh.*]

HOSSEFROSSE and MRS. PAMPINELLI, together.

> HOSSEFROSSE. Yes, I think I had.

> MRS. PAMPINELLI. [*Up at the left, addressing the stage manager*] Are you ready, Mr. Stage Manager? [*He continues to read.*]

HOSSEFROSSE and MRS. PAMPINELLI, together.

HOSSEFROSSE. [*Brushing his clothes*] I don't think a whisk-broom'd be out of place on this stage, either.

MRS. PAMPINELLI. [*Turning to Spindler, who is still occupied with the stage-screw*] Mr. Spindler, will you come here, please? [*Turning back to the stage manager*] Mr. Stage Manager! [*Spindler goes towards her, and Hossefrosse goes through the left door.*]

STAGE MANAGER. [*Looking up from his paper, very peevishly*] Yes?

MRS. PAMPINELLI. Are you all ready?

STAGE MANAGER and TWILLER, together.

STAGE MANAGER. Yes, sure, I'm all ready. [*He resumes his newspaper.*]

TWILLER. [*Turning sharply to Spindler, who has stopped on his way to Mrs. Pampinelli to call Mrs. Fell's attention to the stage-screw, and to warn her to be careful of it*] Oh, go away! Can't you see we're busy.

MRS. PAMPINELLI. Mr. Spindler!

SPINDLER. [*Stepping briskly to her side*] Yes, mam?

MRS. PAMPINELLI. Come here, please. [*Turning to the stage manager*] Mr. Stage Manager—[*He looks up.*] This young man will give you the cue for the curtain, in case I am not here.

STAGE MANAGER. All right. [*He resumes his newspaper.*]

MRS. PAMPINELLI. [*Turning and coming forward again, holding her skirt up off the floor*] You stand right here, Mr. Spindler, and I'll give you the signal when I'm ready.

SPINDLER. All right.

MRS. PAMPINELLI. [*Hurrying towards the left door*] Now, is everybody all right?

FLORENCE. Yes.

MRS. RITTER. I think so.

MRS. PAMPINELLI. How are *you*, Paula?

MRS. RITTER. [*Giggling*] All right.

MRS. PAMPINELLI. Where's Mr. Hossefrosse? [*She glances frantically about.*]

FLORENCE and MRS. RITTER, together.

FLORENCE. He's just stepped on the stage.

MRS. RITTER. He was here a minute ago.

MRS. PAMPINELLI. Mr. Hossefrosse, where are you! [*She opens the left door.*]

MRS. RITTER. [*Calling*] Mr. Hossefrosse! [*He opens the right door and comes out.*]

HOSSEFROSSE. Yes?

TEDDY and MRS. PAMPINELLI, together.

> TEDDY. [*Sitting at the desk over at the right, in the miniature set beyond the flats, to Mrs. Pampinelli, as she comes through the left door*] There he is.
>
> MRS. PAMPINELLI. [*To Teddy, as she steps into the miniature set, through the left door*] Where's Mr. Hossefrosse?

FLORENCE and MRS. RITTER, together.

> FLORENCE. [*To Hossefrosse*] Mrs. Pampinelli's looking for you.
>
> MRS. RITTER. [*Calling*] Here he is, Mrs. Pampinelli! [*Hossefrosse steps quickly to the left door and starts in, just as Mrs. Pampinelli comes out through the right door. Florence steps over to the left door and catches Hossefrosse by the arm, and pulls him back.*]

MRS. PAMPINELLI. [*Coming through the right door*] Where *is* he?

MRS. RITTER. [*Pointing to Hossefrosse*] There he is! [*She laughs.*]

FLORENCE. [*Drawing Hossefrosse back*] Mrs. Pampinelli wants you!

HOSSEFROSSE. [*To Mrs. Pampinelli*] I beg your pardon.

MRS. PAMPINELLI. Oh, Mr. Hossefrosse!

HOSSEFROSSE. [*Crossing to the right towards her*] Yes?

MRS. PAMPINELLI. Are you all right?

HOSSEFROSSE. I think so, yes.

MRS. PAMPINELLI. How is your make-up?

HOSSEFROSSE. All right, I think.

MRS. PAMPINELLI. [*Indicating the right door*] Would you stand here for a moment under this light until I see it?

HOSSEFROSSE. Certainly. [*He goes to the right door and stands with his back against it. The light from the row of electric bulbs over the door shines down on his face. Mrs. Pampinelli stands off to his right, surveying his make-up critically.*]

MRS. PAMPINELLI. Very good.

HOSSEFROSSE. Not too much red?

MRS. PAMPINELLI. No, I shouldn't say so.

HOSSEFROSSE. [*Indicating his right cheek*] Up here, I mean.

MRS. PAMPINELLI. No, I think the contour of your face requires it. It heightens the expression. [*She starts across towards the left.*] It's very good. [*Hossefrosse comes over and chats with the ladies about his make-up.*] Mr. Twiller! [*Twiller turns from Mrs. Fell.*]

TWILLER. Yes? [*Turning back to Mrs. Fell*] Excuse me, Nelly.

MRS. FELL. Certainly.

MRS. PAMPINELLI. How is your mustache?

TWILLER. [*Touching it gingerly*] All right, I think.

MRS. PAMPINELLI. Is it quite secure?

TWILLER. I think so. [*Mrs. Ritter, Florence and Hossefrosse turn and look.*]

MRS. PAMPINELLI. [*Stepping back a step from him and looking at the mustache, with her head tilted a bit to the left side*] You've made it a little smaller, haven't you?

TWILLER. [*Touching the left side of his mustache*] I cut it down a bit on this side.

MRS. PAMPINELLI. I thought you had.

TWILLER. I was a little conscious of it.

MRS. PAMPINELLI. Well,—I don't know but that it's better for the characterization.

TWILLER. And how are my eyes? [*He turns and looks out and away off, widening his eyes as though he were having his picture taken.*]

MRS. PAMPINELLI. [*After looking keenly at his eyes for a second*] Very effective. [*She turns quickly away towards the right, and Twiller turns back to his left to Mrs. Fell.*] Now, is everybody ready? [*They all smile and nod.*] Your gloves and cane, Mr. Hossefrosse?

HOSSEFROSSE. [*Crossing above Florence and Mrs. Ritter towards Mrs. Pampinelli, extending his cane and gloves*] Yes.

MRS. PAMPINELLI. [*Turning towards Mrs. Fell*] Places, Nelly! Get ready, Mr. Spindler!

SPINDLER. I'm all ready. [*Mrs. Fell closes the manuscript, excuses herself to Twiller, and crosses, above him, towards the right. He goes back at the left and says something to Spindler, then comes forward again.*]

MRS. PAMPINELLI. [*Calling through the left door*] Are you all right, Teddy?

TEDDY. [*Beyond the flats, over at the right*] All right. [*As Mrs. Fell passes above Florence and Mrs. Ritter, on her way over to the right, she whispers something to them which causes a general laugh:—then she continues on over to the door at the right and takes up her official position, as promptress.*]

MRS. PAMPINELLI. [*Turning and addressing them generally*] Now, is everybody all right? [*They all nod.*] You both all right, girls? [*Mrs. Ritter nods.*]

FLORENCE. All right.

MRS. PAMPINELLI. [*Turning around to the left to Mr. Spindler, and with an authoritative gesture*] All right, then—take up the curtain!

SPINDLER. [*Waving his hand to the stage manager*] All right, Stage Manager!

STAGE MANAGER. [*Getting up, very reluctantly*] Are you ready?

MRS. PAMPINELLI and SPINDLER, together.

    MRS. PAMPINELLI. Yes, all ready.

    SPINDLER. Let her go!

MRS. PAMPINELLI. [*With a kind of ceremonious flourish of the hand*] Take up the curtain! [*The stage manager tosses his newspaper onto the chair and steps out of sight, to the left. There is an anxious pause. Then Mrs. Pampinelli starts violently and grabs the knob of the left door.*] Oh, wait one moment! [*Spindler rushes back at the left, whistling.*]

FLORENCE, MRS. RITTER, TWILLER and HOSSEFROSSE, together, [*as Mrs. Pampinelli pulls open the left door.*]

    FLORENCE. Wait a minute!

    MRS. RITTER. Oh, wait!

    TWILLER. Hold it!

    HOSSEFROSSE. [*Grabbing the door and holding it open*] Not yet!

MRS. RITTER. [*Calling to the stage manager*] Just a minute!

MRS. PAMPINELLI. [*Going in through the left door*] One moment, please! [*She vanishes to the right, and there is a slight pause, during which the curtain, which had been raised four feet, can be seen through the door to descend again. They all exchange looks of*

distress and amused annoyance. Then Mrs. Pampinelli hurries out through the door again.]
All right!

SPINDLER. [*Who has come forward at the left*] Is it all right? [*Hossefrosse releases the door and it closes.*]

MRS. PAMPINELLI. Yes, it's all right. [*Spindler goes towards the back at the left and she follows him half-way.*]

SPINDLER. All right, Mr. Stage Manager!

STAGE MANAGER. [*Off at the left*] Are you ready?

MRS. PAMPINELLI and SPINDLER, together.

      MRS. PAMPINELLI. Yes, all ready, Mr. Stage Manager!

      SPINDLER. Let her go!

MRS. PAMPINELLI. [*Turning and coming forward at the left*] Take it up! [*She stands just to the left of the left door, peering through the flats. Spindler is farther back at the left, peering, also; and Mrs. Fell is over at the right door, peering. There is a pause. Mr. Hossefrosse takes up his position outside the left door, preparatory to making his entrance. He settles his clothes generally, and clears his throat.*] The curtain is going up, Mr. Hossefrosse, go on.

HOSSEFROSSE. Is it up?

MRS. PAMPINELLI. Yes, yes, go on! [*He opens the door, rather magnificently, and swings in. There is a ripple of applause, and the door closes after him; and they all try to find a crevice between the flats that will afford a glimpse of the stage beyond. The stage manager appears from the left carrying a regulation door-slam, which he brings forward and drops, with a bang, just to the left of the left door. They all turn and look at him, in resentful astonishment, but he simply gives them a look of infinite disdain and returns to his chair at the back to read.*]

HOSSEFROSSE. [*Beyond the flats*] Anybody here, David?

TEDDY. [*Beyond the flats, over toward the right*] No, sir.

HOSSEFROSSE. [*Beyond the flats, moving towards the right*] No telephones?

TEDDY. No, sir.

HOSSEFROSSE. [*Coming through the right door, without his hat*] Nothing at all, eh? [*Mrs. Ritter is standing right in front of the door.*]

MRS. PAMPINELLI. Get away from the door, Paula! [*Paula jumps to the left. Mrs. Fell takes advantage of the crevice caused by the door being open, to try to see the audience.*]

TEDDY. [*Who can be seen through the open door standing at the desk*] No, sir.

HOSSEFROSSE. [*Leaning over and laying his cane and gloves on the chair between the doors*] All right, sir. [*The door begins to swing to behind him.*]

MRS. PAMPINELLI. Keep that door open, Mr. Hossefrosse! [*Spindler comes forward at the left to see what's the matter. Hossefrosse thrusts his foot back and kicks the door open.*]

HOSSEFROSSE. And I think that will do very nicely for this day. [*The door begins slowly to swing to again.*]

MRS. PAMPINELLI. There it goes again, Mr. Hossefrosse!

HOSSEFROSSE. It won't *stay* open! [*Mrs. Fell looks around the door.*]

MRS. PAMPINELLI. Take hold of that door, Nelly! [*Nelly puts one foot around it, and stands looking at her manuscript. Spindler goes back at the left and looks through the wings again, at the stage.*]

HOSSEFROSSE. [*In a frantic whisper*] Telephone!

MRS. FELL. Telephone, somebody!

HOSSEFROSSE. Good Lord!

FLORENCE. Mr. Spindler, telephone! [*Spindler rushes forward at the left.*]

MRS. PAMPINELLI. Where is he?

SPINDLER. What?

FLORENCE. The telephone-bell!

MRS. PAMPINELLI. Where's your bell?

SPINDLER. [*Pulling the battery-arrangement out of his pocket*] Has the cue been given?

TEDDY. [*Picking up the telephone on the desk beyond the flats*] Hello?

MRS. PAMPINELLI. Ring it! Of course it's been given! [*He rings the bell, and Hossefrosse steps through the right door and watches Teddy anxiously.*]

SPINDLER. I didn't hear it!

MRS. PAMPINELLI. [*Annihilating him with a look, and starting over towards the right door*] Well, why aren't you over here when your cue's given and then you would hear it! [*Spindler trails over after her.*]

HOSSEFROSSE. [*Over his shoulder, to Mrs. Pampinelli*] Shush!

MRS. PAMPINELLI. [*Turning sharply back towards the left, and directly to Spindler, who is right behind her*] Shush! [*She passes below him and continues towards the left.*] Keep away from that door, they'll see you! [*In attempting to keep out of the way of the door, Spindler turns sharply and trips over the screw of a stage-brace, falling his length across the open door. Mrs. Ritter gives a little scream, and Mrs. Pampinelli whirls round and glares at him. He scrambles to his feet, and Mrs. Ritter giggles and pulls him to the left, away from the door.*]

HOSSEFROSSE. [*Standing in the open door, addressing Teddy*] Mrs. A.? [*Teddy nods, and Hossefrosse pretends to pick up an imaginary telephone from a desk just to the left of the right door.*] Yes? All right. [*He pretends to hang up and set the telephone down on the desk again.*] You can clear out of here now, David, any time you like,— Mrs. Arlington is on her way up.

TEDDY. [*Rising, and settling the various papers on the desk*] All right.

MRS. RITTER. [*Helping Mr. Spindler to brush off his clothes*] Did you hurt yourself, Mr. Spindler? [*Mrs. Pampinelli tries to attract Spindler's attention to the door-slam.*]

SPINDLER. No. [*He hurries over to the door-slam at the left and picks it up.*]

HOSSEFROSSE. I'll let you off early Monday. [*Florence stands anxiously outside the left door.*]

TEDDY. Oh, that's all right.

HOSSEFROSSE. And don't forget to leave that list with the Robinson people on your way down Monday.

TEDDY. No, sir, I won't; I have it right here in me pocket. [*Florence puts her lips against the left door and coughs hard. Then she shuffles her feet; so does Spindler. Hossefrosse steps through the right door and looks over toward the left door.*]

HOSSEFROSSE. [*Addressing Teddy, in a subdued tone*] Is that someone coming?

TEDDY. [*Looking toward the left door*] I think so. [*There is a slight pause, then Mrs. Pampinelli makes a decisive movement to Spindler and he brings the door-slam down with a thunderous bang. Mrs. Pampinelli starts violently.*]

MRS. PAMPINELLI. That's too loud, Mr. Spindler!

SPINDLER. There's too much wood in it! [*He starts across to the right.*]

HOSSEFROSSE. [*Stepping down to Teddy's desk and picking up his hat*] That can't be Mrs. Arlington already. I won't see anyone else. [*He starts back towards the door.*] Tell them I've gone; and don't let anybody wait. [*He takes hold of the door as he steps through.*] Say you're just locking up the office. [*He comes through the door and tries to close it, but Nelly's foot is still around it, and she is lost in the manuscript. He pulls at the door, but she is oblivious.*]

MRS. RITTER. Nelly! [*Spindler gives a little whistle to attract her attention.*]

MRS. PAMPINELLI. Let go of the door, Nelly!

MRS. FELL. [*Jumping out of the way, to the right*] Oh, I beg your pardon! [*Hossefrosse scowls at her and closes the door. Spindler jumps to the door and turns a key, which he has in his hand, in the lock, then touches the button at the end of the cord, extinguishing the row of lights over the door, then rushes back towards the left door. Mrs. Ritter is right in his way as he rushes back, and they dodge each other twice before Mr. Spindler can get past. When he reaches the left door, he raps violently, Mrs. Pampinelli directing his activities with little nervous gestures. There is a pause: then the left door is opened by Teddy. Mrs. Ritter is right in front of it.*]

MRS. PAMPINELLI. [*Standing to the left of the door*] Get out of the way, Paula! [*Mrs. Ritter jumps out of the way, to the right, then looks back at Mrs. Pampinelli and giggles, but Mrs. Pampinelli puts her finger on her lips.*]

FLORENCE. [*Passing through the left door*] Good evening, son.

TEDDY. [*Reaching out and closing the door*] Good evening. [*There is prolonged applause from beyond the flats, and everybody, having seen Florence safely through the door, rushes to his favorite crevice between the wings, or rip in the scenery, to see how she is being received by the audience.*]

FLORENCE. [*Beyond the flats*] Isn't the Doctor in?

TEDDY. No, mam, he ain't; he went about six o'clock.

FLORENCE. That's unfortunate, I wanted to see him. [*Hossefrosse turns away from the right door, where he's been peeking, and mops his brow: then he turns and puts his hat down on the chair.*]

SPINDLER. [*Stepping towards him from the left door*] How do you feel?

HOSSEFROSSE. All right; but that door and that telephone got me kind of rattled.

MRS. PAMPINELLI. [*Looking over from the extreme left of the back flat, where she has been peeking*] Shush, boys! [*Hossefrosse turns away and tiptoes towards the right, and the others resume their peeking.*]

MRS. FELL. [*Turning to Hossefrosse, as he passes below her*] What's the matter, Huxley, did something go wrong? [*Mrs. Pampinelli looks over again to see who's talking.*]

HOSSEFROSSE. [*Indicating the right door*] That door kind of got me rattled for a minute.

MRS. FELL. I don't think the audience noticed it.

MRS. PAMPINELLI. Shush! [*Nelly consults her manuscript, listening at the same time to the dialogue beyond the flats, and Mr. Hossefrosse continues to the extreme right and forward, trying to make the squeak of his new shoes as inaudible as possible. Mrs. Pampinelli puts her ear to the flat and listens keenly.*]

TEDDY. [*Faintly, beyond the flats*] Why, he always asts me to wait whenever he's expectin' his wife downtown. [*Spindler suddenly turns from the wing where he has been peeking, and, breaking into quite a jaunty little whistle, starts across towards the left; but Mrs. Pampinelli turns abruptly and glares him into silence. He clasps his hand over his mouth and apologizes with an obsequious little gesture.*]

FLORENCE. [*Beyond the flats*] I see. And he was expecting her this evening?

TEDDY. Yes, mam.

FLORENCE. Do you know her? [*Spindler trips and almost falls over the stage-screw in the floor at the left. Twiller, who has been standing down at the extreme left, makes an impatient move and goes up towards the back.*]

MRS. PAMPINELLI. Oh, Mr. Spindler, for Pity's sake do keep still for one moment!

SPINDLER. [*Squatting down and attempting to remove the screw*] We'd better get this thing out of here, before somebody gets hurt.

MRS. PAMPINELLI. Now, don't take that out of there, Mr. Spindler! You might loosen the scenery.

SPINDLER. This isn't connected with the scenery.

MRS. PAMPINELLI. You don't know whether it is or not! Leave it where it is.

SPINDLER. [*Getting up and moving over towards the right*] Somebody's going to get their neck broken, the first thing you know.

MRS. PAMPINELLI. Very well, then, that will be their misfortune! We've simply got to be careful, that's all. Get ready, Paula. [*Mrs. Ritter giggles and takes up her position outside the left door.*]

MRS. FELL. [*As Spindler comes towards her*] What's the matter, Mr. Spindler?

SPINDLER. [*In quite a temper, and indicating the stage-screw over at the left*] Why, that thing there is sticking right up in the middle of the floor, and the first thing you—

MRS. PAMPINELLI. Shush!—[*He turns and scowls at her, and she glares at him. He passes below Mrs. Fell and over to Hossefrosse, at the extreme right and forward, where he whispers his grievance.*]

MRS. FELL. You all right, Paula? [*Paula nods yes.*]

MRS. PAMPINELLI. Don't be nervous, now, Paula. [*Twiller comes forward at the left.*]

MRS. RITTER. I'm not the least bit, dear, really.

MRS. PAMPINELLI. Well, that's splendid, dear. I'll open the door for you. [*She takes hold of the knob of the left door.*]

MRS. RITTER. All right, thank you. [*They stand listening, keenly.*]

FLORENCE. [*Beyond the flats*] Do you mind if I wait a few minutes, in case he comes?

TEDDY. [*Beyond the flats*] Why, I was just going home.

FLORENCE. Oh, were you? [*Twiller lifts his hat and gives it a little wave at Mrs. Ritter, and she waves her hand back at him.*]

TEDDY. Yes, mam; and I have to lock up the office before I go.

MRS. PAMPINELLI. [*Suddenly*] There it is now, dear. [*She opens the door, and Mrs. Ritter steps back a bit, in order to make a more effective entrance.*] Good luck, darling.

MRS. RITTER. [*Turning to her*] Thank you, dear. [*She steps through the door, tripping awkwardly over the door-strip. Mrs. Pampinelli makes a gesture of extreme annoyance. There is an outburst of applause; then Mrs. Pampinelli closes the door, and they all step to the flats and peek through, Mrs. Pampinelli at the left door, Mrs. Fell at the right, Mr. Spindler between them, and Hossefrosse and Twiller about half-way back at the right and left, respectively. There is a pause; and then Mrs. Ritter can be heard beyond the flats.*] Hello, kid!

TEDDY. Hello, Mrs. Arlington.

MRS. RITTER. Is my sweetie in?

TEDDY. No, mam, he ain't.

MRS. RITTER. [*With an unnatural inflection*] What!

MRS. FELL. [*Calling over in a whisper to Mrs. Pampinelli*] Betty! [*Mrs. Pampinelli doesn't hear her, so she tiptoes over towards her.*] Betty!

MRS. PAMPINELLI. What?

MRS. FELL. Did Paula trip?

MRS. PAMPINELLI. [*Coming away from the flat, and moving down to Mrs. Fell*] Yes. [*Mrs. Fell gives an annoyed shake of her head.*] But I don't see how anyone can get onto *that* stage *without* tripping.

MRS. FELL. I don't either.

MRS. PAMPINELLI. It seems an utter impossibility to me for anyone, especially a woman, to get through those doors without catching her heel or her skirt or something. [*Spindler crosses to the left, back of the ladies, and speaks to Twiller.*]

MRS. FELL. [*Returning to the right door*] It's dreadful!

MRS. PAMPINELLI. [*Turning to her left and going back again to the left door*] I don't see the necessity of it.

MRS. FELL. [*Opening her manuscript*] I don't either.

MRS. PAMPINELLI. [*Listening keenly*] I'm afraid they're not hearing Paula at all.

MRS. FELL. What?

MRS. PAMPINELLI. I say, I'm afraid Paula isn't loud enough.

MRS. FELL. Well, why don't you speak to her, Betty, she's sitting right here. [*She indicates the point right inside the right door, and Mrs. Pampinelli, picking up her skirt, hurries over. Mrs. Fell steps out of the way, to the right.*]

MRS. PAMPINELLI. [*Putting her lips to the joining of the door-wing and the side wing*] Speak a little louder, Paula! I'm afraid they're not hearing you!

MRS. FELL. Can she hear you?

MRS. PAMPINELLI. A little louder, dear! [*The right door is thrust open by Teddy.*]

TEDDY. [*In a frantic whisper*] There's no pen and ink on the desk! [*Spindler rushes over from the left.*]

SPINDLER. What? [*Mrs. Pampinelli, Mrs. Fell and Mr. Hossefrosse rush round to him from the right.*]

TEDDY. No pen and ink!

MRS. PAMPINELLI. What is it, Teddy?

TEDDY and SPINDLER, together.

>TEDDY. No pen and ink on the desk!

>SPINDLER. No pen and ink!

MRS. PAMPINELLI. My God!

MRS. FELL. Tell her to use a lead-pencil!

TEDDY and MRS. PAMPINELLI, together.

>TEDDY.—[*To Mrs. Fell*] There's none on there!

>MRS. PAMPINELLI. Give him a lead-pencil, Mr. Spindler!

SPINDLER. [*Whirling and springing towards the left*] Haven't got one! [*Teddy, Mrs. Pampinelli and Mrs. Fell rush after him.*]

SPINDLER and MRS. PAMPINELLI, together.

>SPINDLER. Twiller!

MRS. PAMPINELLI. Oh, dear, dear!

TWILLER. [*Rushing towards them from the left*] What's the matter?

SPINDLER and TEDDY, together.

> SPINDLER. Got a lead-pencil?
>
> TEDDY. Give him a lead-pencil, Ralph!

TWILLER. [*Dropping his cane*] No! [*They fling him out of the way, to the left, and rush on back to the stage manager.*] What are you trying to do, knock me off my feet!

MRS. PAMPINELLI. Haven't you got one, Mr. Twiller?

SPINDLER and MRS. FELL, together.

> SPINDLER. [*To the stage manager*] Got a lead-pencil, old man?
>
> MRS. FELL. [*At Mrs. Pampinelli's heels*] There's one in my bag somewhere!

MRS. PAMPINELLI, SPINDLER and TEDDY, together.

> MRS. PAMPINELLI. [*Turning to Mrs. Fell*] See what they're doing out there, Nelly!
>
> SPINDLER. [*To the stage manager*] Or a fountain-pen!
>
> TEDDY. [*To the stage manager*] They need it on the stage!

MRS. FELL and STAGE MANAGER, together.

> MRS. FELL. [*Turning and rushing back towards the right door*] Certainly, darling!
>
> STAGE MANAGER. [*Feeling in his shirt-pockets*] Well, now, wait a minute, wait a minute!

MRS. FELL. [*Turning with a despairing gesture, after having opened the right door and looked in*] My dear, they're not doing a thing, they're just sitting there!

MRS. PAMPINELLI. [*Turning to the left*] Hurry, boys! [*Turning to the right*] Tell them to say something, Nelly! Anything at all! Something about the weather! [*Nelly runs to the extreme right end of the flat. Teddy and Spindler come rushing forward at the left.*] Did you get it, Teddy?

TEDDY and SPINDLER, together.

> TEDDY. Yes!
>
> SPINDLER. Yes, he's got it!

MRS. PAMPINELLI. [*Indicating the left door*] Go on here, Teddy! [*He grabs the knob of the door, but it won't open.*]

MRS. FELL. [*Calling through the flats*] Say something, Paula!

MRS. PAMPINELLI. You should never leave the stage during a scene, Teddy!

TEDDY and MRS. FELL, together.

> TEDDY. [*Wrestling with the door*] Damn these doors!
>
> MRS. FELL. [*Calling through the flats*] Something about the weather!

MRS. PAMPINELLI. Take hold of this, Mr. Spindler! [*He grabs the knob of the door and Teddy runs across to the right door.*]

TEDDY. I'll go on here!

MRS. FELL. [*As Teddy goes through the right door*] If you can't use one door, use the other! [*The door closes after him; and Mrs. Pampinelli turns and looks upon Spindler, who is still trying to get the left door open.*]

MRS. PAMPINELLI. You know, this is *all your fault*, Mr. Spindler. [*He doesn't look up.*] You said you'd attend to all those properties!

MRS. FELL. What's the matter with the door, Betty?

MRS. PAMPINELLI. [*To Spindler*] Never mind it now. [*She moves towards the center of the stage.*]

SPINDLER. We'd better get it open before somebody has to use it again.

MRS. PAMPINELLI. Go away from it, I tell you! [*He walks away towards the left, sulking.*] It will probably open all right from the other side. [*She comes forward slowly, touching her hair and relaxing generally, then, suddenly, stands stock-still, and listens, wide-eyed. She looks quickly at Mrs. Fell, who is carefully settling her necklace, at the right door.*] What's wrong out there, Nelly? [*Nelly turns and looks through the flats, then turns quickly to Mrs. Pampinelli.*]

MRS. FELL. I think he's up!

MRS. PAMPINELLI. [*Frozen to the spot*] Who? [*Nelly looks again, and then back to Mrs. Pampinelli.*]

MRS. FELL. All of them!

MRS. PAMPINELLI. [*Picking up her skirt and rushing towards the right door*] Let me see! [*Nelly jumps out of the way, to the right, and Twiller and Spindler rush to the left door and peek through. Mrs. Pampinelli peeks through, and then speaks through the flats.*] What's the matter, Teddy? Go over and get your hat and coat! [*Turning frantically to Mrs. Fell*] He's up in his lines! What is it?

MRS. FELL. [*In a panic*] Up in his lines!

MRS. PAMPINELLI and MRS. FELL, together.

> MRS. PAMPINELLI. [*Speaking through the flats*] Go over and get your hat and coat, Teddy! Don't stand there like a jack!

> MRS. FELL. [*Handing the manuscript to Hossefrosse, who is at her right*] Oh, find that for me, will you, Huxley! [*He takes the manuscript from her and turns it over furiously, while Nelly opens her lorgnon.*] About page eleven, I think it is! [*She assists him in finding the place.*]

MRS. PAMPINELLI. What was the last line, Nelly? This is dreadful!

MRS. FELL. Now, wait a moment, darling! Don't get me nervous, or I'll *never* be able to find it! [*Twiller and Spindler are in a panic of suspense over at the left door.*]

HOSSEFROSSE. Here's page eleven.

MRS. FELL. Is that eleven? Well, now, here it is, right here— Why, a— I'll get you an envelope!

MRS. PAMPINELLI. What's the next?

MRS. FELL. The next is—a—why a—I've got to go now—

MRS. FELL and MRS. PAMPINELLI, together.

> MRS. FELL. It takes me nearly an hour to get home!

> MRS. PAMPINELLI. [*Calling through the flats*] I've got to go now!

TEDDY and MRS. PAMPINELLI, together.

> TEDDY. [*Beyond the flats*] I've got to go now!

> MRS. PAMPINELLI. [*Calling through the flats*] It takes me nearly an hour to get home.

TEDDY. It takes me an hour to get home!

MRS. FELL. Are they all right?

MRS. PAMPINELLI. [*Coming away from the flats*] Yes, they're all right now. But you'd better stand right here, I'm afraid of Paula. [*She moves towards the left.*]

SPINDLER. [*Coming towards her*] You know, I could have *sworn* I put a pen and ink on that desk!

MRS. PAMPINELLI. [*Imperiously*] Please, Mr. Spindler, don't explain anything! I am interested in results. [*She turns and moves back again towards the right, and*

Spindler goes over to the left. Just as he passes beyond the left door, the entire lock and knob fall to the floor. He turns nervously, only to find Mrs. Pampinelli, who has turned quite as nervously, looking at him dangerously.]

SPINDLER. I didn't *touch* it!

MRS. PAMPINELLI. Will you go away, before you ruin the entire performance! [*He snaps around and goes over to the left and up towards the back.*]

TEDDY. [*Opening the left door and swaying through*] Good night. [*He is dressed in a brown sack-suit and wears tan shoes.*]

FLORENCE. [*Beyond the flats*] Good night, son.

MRS. RITTER. [*Beyond the flats*] Good night, kid.

MRS. PAMPINELLI. [*Going towards him*] You should *never* walk off the stage, Teddy, in the middle of a scene! [*He closes the door behind him, and, pressing his hand to his brow, starts towards the left.*] Do something, no matter what it is! [*He falls backward in a full-length faint. She catches him.*] Oh, dear child! Mr. Spindler! Come here, Mr. Twiller, Teddy's fainted! [*Twiller, who has been standing over at the left, and forward, rushes towards her; and Mrs. Fell, followed by Hossefrosse, comes rushing from the right.*]

MRS. FELL. [*In a panic*] What's the matter, Betty!

MRS. PAMPINELLI. Take Teddy over to the door, Mr. Twiller, he's fainted!

TWILLER. [*Dropping his cane, in his excitement*] I *can't* take him now, I've got a cue coming right here in a minute! [*Spindler comes rushing down from the left.*]

MRS. PAMPINELLI. Here, Mr. Spindler, take Teddy over to the door, where he'll get some air! He's sick. Look at the color of him. [*She hands him to Spindler, who half carries him up at the left; and she and Twiller follow on behind them.*] Hold on to him, now, Mr. Spindler.

MRS. FELL. [*Turning back towards the right door, and addressing Hossefrosse, who has returned to his former position down at the right*] I always said he wasn't strong enough for that part! [*She just gets past the right door when it is frantically opened and Mrs. Ritter thrusts her head out.*]

MRS. RITTER. [*Breathlessly*] Mr. Twiller! [*The door closes again.*]

MRS. FELL. [*Running towards the left*] Mr. Twiller! They're waiting for you!

MRS. PAMPINELLI. [*Rushing forward at the left*] What is it?

MRS. FELL. [*In a perfect frenzy*] They're waiting for Mr. Twiller!

MRS. PAMPINELLI. Mr. Twiller! [*He snatches up his cane from the floor, but the hook of it catches in the stage-brace, and he has considerable yanking to do to get it loose. Mrs.*

Fell raps on the left door.] Go on, Mr. Twiller, for Heaven's sake! the stage is waiting! [*She pulls the door open for him. He straightens his hat and then raps on the wing beside the door.*] Oh, go on! never mind rapping! that's been done! [*He steps through the door and she slams it after him, catching his left arm and hand. The cane is in his left hand, and it falls at Mrs. Pampinelli's feet. She pulls the door open again to release his arm; then gives the door a definite slam. A burst of applause greets Twiller's entrance. Mrs. Pampinelli is in a perfect wrath. She sweeps across towards the right, and back again all the way across to the left; then turns and starts back towards the right. As she passes the left door she sees Twiller's cane, and, realizing in a flash that he will have need of it in his scene, she picks it up, opens the left door slightly, and flings it in onto the stage. Then she continues on towards the right, turns and crosses back again to the left, holding up her skirt and bristling with temper.*]

MRS. FELL. [*Back at the right door, speaking to Hossefrosse, down at the right*] How are my eyes? Instead of paying attention to his part!

MRS. PAMPINELLI. [*Coming across to the right*] People rehearsing their cues a thousand times, and then don't know them when they hear them! It's positively disgusting! [*She turns and goes back again to the left, turns, and starts back to the right. Hossefrosse tiptoes towards her.*]

HOSSEFROSSE. What happened to Teddy, did he get sick out there?

MRS. PAMPINELLI. No, just a little reaction. [*Hossefrosse nods comprehendingly.*] He gives too much to the scene. He doesn't understand emotional conservation yet. [*Hossefrosse shakes his head knowingly and returns to the right, and Mrs. Pampinelli steps to the left door and listens.*]

FLORENCE. [*Just audibly, beyond the flats*] She's waiting for my very unpunctual husband. In fact, we are both waiting for him, to be precise. But I've just been telling her I'm afraid we may as well give it up, for he's never kept an appointment in his life. I'm sorry he isn't here, if you wanted to see him.

TWILLER. [*Beyond the flats*] I don't know whether I wanted to see him or not; it depends.

FLORENCE. I don't understand you.

TWILLER. I don't fully understand myself! [*There is a very general laugh from beyond the flats. Mrs. Pampinelli looks anxiously at Nelly, and Nelly looks up at her from the manuscript.*]

MRS. PAMPINELLI. What was *that?*

MRS. FELL. [*Not having caught what she said*] What?

MRS. PAMPINELLI. What was that the audience was laughing at? [*Mrs. Fell peeks through at the door where she is standing, then turns desperately to Mrs. Pampinelli.*]

MRS. FELL. Half of Mr. Twiller's mustache fell off! [*She looks through the peek again. Mrs. Pampinelli puts her hand against her brow and leans upon the stage-brace, the picture of tragedy. Mrs. Fell turns to her again.*] I don't think the audience noticed it, he stuck it right on again!

MRS. PAMPINELLI. That doesn't matter, there is absolutely no excuse for it! He's been here since four o'clock this afternoon! [*She crosses towards the left and back again.*]

FLORENCE. [*Beyond the flats*] What sort of a rumor was it, Mr. Rush, if I may ask?

TWILLER. [*Beyond the flats*] The usual kind. [*There's another laugh from beyond the flats, and Mrs. Pampinelli stands petrified, just below the left door. Mrs. Fell turns quickly and peeks, then turns to Mrs. Pampinelli.*]

MRS. FELL. [*Despairingly*] It fell off again! [*Mrs. Pampinelli raises her fists and shakes them.*]

MRS. PAMPINELLI. Well, why on earth hasn't he brains enough to leave it off!

MRS. FELL. He has his hat on, too! [*Mrs. Pampinelli steps to the left door and speaks through it.*]

MRS. PAMPINELLI. Leave your mustache *off*, Mr. Twiller! Leave it *off*!—And take off your *hat*, you're inside. [*Hossefrosse tiptoes over from the right.*]

HOSSEFROSSE. What's the matter, did his mustache fall off?

MRS. PAMPINELLI. Yes, twice; and he keeps sticking it on again. [*He shakes his head regretfully and tiptoes back to the right.*]

MRS. RITTER. [*Beyond the flats*] It's perfectly ridiculous!

FLORENCE. [*Beyond the flats*] Too bad my husband isn't here.

TWILLER. [*Beyond the flats*] Yes, it is; I had counted upon seeing him.

FLORENCE. I'm sure he'd be able to explain.

TWILLER. Well, I hope he would!—the thing is damned annoying! [*Mrs. Ritter gives an unearthly laugh, which is supposed to express derision. Mrs. Fell looks up from her manuscript, and Mrs. Pampinelli smiles and nods approvingly at her.*] Even if *you* don't appreciate it!

MRS. FELL. Wonderful. [*She turns and smiles and nods at Hossefrosse; then they all listen again. The stage manager, who has arisen from his chair at the sound of Mrs. Ritter's disdainful laughter, comes forward at the left, with his pipe in one hand and his newspaper in the other. He has a puzzled, inquiring expression, and looks from one to the other quizzically; but Mrs. Pampinelli has her back to him, Mrs. Fell is looking at her*] manuscript, and Mr. Hossefrosse's face is, as usual, utterly expressionless, so he steps to the juncture of the back flats with the side wings and peeks through, curiously. Then he returns to his chair up at the left, shaking his head from side to side.]

MRS. RITTER. [*Beyond the flats*] I don't know what it is, yet!

TWILLER. [*Beyond the flats*] You know very well what it is!

MRS. RITTER. You haven't told us.

TWILLER. You're here, aren't you!

MRS. RITTER. Yes.

TWILLER. Well, that's it, exactly! [*Mrs. Pampinelli smiles approvingly, and moves towards the right.*]

MRS. PAMPINELLI. [*Calling Hossefrosse, who is engaged in studying his lines from a paper, over at the right*] Mr. Hossefrosse.

MRS. FELL. [*Turning to him*] Huxley! [*He looks up, and tiptoes towards Mrs. Pampinelli.*]

MRS. PAMPINELLI. How is this hall to speak in?

HOSSEFROSSE. Why, I shouldn't say it was good.

MRS. PAMPINELLI. I thought not.

HOSSEFROSSE. It's too big for the speaking voice.

MRS. PAMPINELLI. [*With a gesture*] You have to *project* the tone, do you not?

HOSSEFROSSE. Oh, yes, absolutely.

MRS. PAMPINELLI. [*Taking a step towards the back flat, and listening*] I'm afraid they're not hearing Paula at all.

HOSSEFROSSE. [*Putting his fingers to his throat*] I'm using my upper register almost entirely.

MRS. PAMPINELLI. [*Glancing at him*] You're very fortunate to know how to do it.

HOSSEFROSSE. Did it sound all right from back here?

MRS. PAMPINELLI. Oh, splendid, yes, Mr. Hossefrosse!—your voice is beautiful. [*He raises his hand deprecatingly.*] Really,—I was just saying to Mrs. Fell, I'm so sorry there isn't another act, that you might sing a solo between them. [*He beams and deprecates again, profusely, and turns to the right. Spindler comes down at the left and towards Mrs. Pampinelli.*] Really! Splendid. [*She sees Spindler.*] Where's Teddy?

SPINDLER. He's gone over to the drug store.

MRS. PAMPINELLI. With his make-up on?

SPINDLER. He said he wanted to get some aromatic spirits of ammonia.

MRS. PAMPINELLI. You have a cue right here soon, haven't you?

SPINDLER. [*Taking the telephone-arrangement from his pocket, and crossing towards the right door*] Where are they?

MRS. FELL. [*Suddenly looking up from her manuscript*] Telephone, Mr. Spindler!

MRS. PAMPINELLI. There it is now, ring it!

SPINDLER. [*Shaking it desperately*] It won't ring! [*Mrs. Fell turns to Hossefrosse in desperation.*]

MRS. PAMPINELLI, MRS. FELL and HOSSEFROSSE, together.

>   MRS. PAMPINELLI. Shake it harder, it rang before!

>   MRS. FELL. What's the matter with the fool thing!

>   HOSSEFROSSE. Hit it against something, Mr. Spindler!

SPINDLER. There's something the matter with the battery!

FLORENCE. [*Audibly, from beyond the flats*] Hello!

MRS. PAMPINELLI. [*Relaxing*] Let it go,—it's too late now. [*Spindler continues to tinker with it.*] You've missed every other cue, [*She moves towards the left.*] you may as well be consistent for the rest of the evening.

SPINDLER. [*Following her*] Well, good night! I can't help it if the electricity won't work, can I?

MRS. PAMPINELLI. [*Turning upon him furiously*] You should have attended to it beforehand and then it *would* work! [*Mrs. Fell waves her hand at them, to be quiet.*]

SPINDLER. Well, My God! I can't be in a half-a-dozen places at the same time!

MRS. FELL. Shush! [*Hossefrosse tiptoes up to her and deplores the noise that Mrs. Pampinelli and Spindler are making.*]

MRS. PAMPINELLI. No one is asking you to be in half-a-dozen places at the same time! You've simply been asked to attend to your cues; and you've missed every one you've had!

MRS. FELL and HOSSEFROSSE, together. Shush!

SPINDLER. You told me to take care of Teddy, didn't you?

MRS. PAMPINELLI. I told you to take him to the door! I *didn't* say to take him all the way to the drug store!

SPINDLER. Did you want me to let the man wander off somewhere by himself, and maybe die!

MRS. FELL. [*Waving her manuscript at them*] Shus—sh!

MRS. PAMPINELLI and SPINDLER, together.

>SPINDLER. Just for the sake of not missing a cue!

>MRS. PAMPINELLI. [*With bitter amusement*] There is very little danger of his dying! And even if he did die, your duty is here! [*She points to the floor with an imperative gesture. The right door is quietly pushed open, and Twiller, with one-half of his mustache gone, pokes his head out.*]

TWILLER. Shush! [*He glances from one side to the other, withdraws his head, and quietly closes the door. Spindler crosses below Mrs. Pampinelli, to the left, then turns and looks at her angrily.*]

MRS. FELL. [*Turning to Hossefrosse*] What did I tell you! Making more noise out here than they are out there!

MRS. PAMPINELLI. [*Still holding her gesture, but following Spindler with her eyes*] Performances are never interrupted simply because one of the artists happens to die! If you were a professional you'd know that; but you're not! [*She turns away from him, towards the right, and, simultaneously, the left door is opened, almost striking her. She raises her arm to protect herself. Mrs. Ritter is standing in the doorway.*]

MRS. RITTER. [*Speaking to Twiller, who is still beyond the flats*] Look and see. [*The telephone-arrangement in Spindler's hands suddenly rings wildly.*]

MRS. PAMPINELLI. [*Turning to him frantically*] Oh, stop that thing! [*Mrs. Ritter glances furtively over her left shoulder at Mrs. Pampinelli. Mrs. Fell comes rushing over, motioning to Spindler to stop the bell.*]

SPINDLER. [*Struggling with the bell*] I can't stop it! [*Mrs. Ritter hastily steps back through the door and pulls it to after her.*]

MRS. PAMPINELLI. Well, then, take it outside, where they can't hear it! [*Spindler scrambles towards the back and out of sight at the left. Mrs. Pampinelli starts back towards the right.*]

MRS. FELL. What's the matter with that Spindler man, anyway!

MRS. PAMPINELLI. I don't know what's the matter with him! I've given up thinking about him.

MRS. FELL. He acts to me like a person that wouldn't be in his right mind! [*She goes back towards the right door.*]

MRS. PAMPINELLI. [*Standing in the middle of the stage*] He's simply not a professional, that's all. [*The left door opens again and Mrs. Ritter is standing in it. Mrs. Pampinelli turns suddenly and looks at her. Mrs. Ritter repeats her unearthly laugh, which again arouses the curiosity of the stage manager, to the extent that he rises and comes forward again at the left to get a look at her. Then he returns to his chair, taking the door-slam with him, and standing it against the wing.*]

MRS. RITTER. [*Addressing Twiller, beyond the flats*] What about the gentlemen?

FLORENCE. [*Beyond the flats*] Jealous husbands, chiefly, aren't they? [*Twiller comes out through the left door, past Mrs. Ritter.*] Didn't you want to leave a message for the Doctor, Mr. Rush? [*Twiller turns right round and goes back to the door.*]

TWILLER. Who, me?

FLORENCE. If you wish.

MRS. RITTER. [*Having some difficulty seeing Florence over Twiller's right shoulder*] He might leave an apology.

MRS. PAMPINELLI. [*Very much annoyed, and stepping close to the flat, just to the right of the door*] Get out of the doorway, Mr. Twiller!

FLORENCE. [*Beyond the flats*] Perhaps we haven't convinced him of his mistake.

MRS. PAMPINELLI and MRS. RITTER, together.

> MRS. PAMPINELLI. [*Trying desperately to attract Twiller's attention, and becoming more emphatic*] Get out of the doorway, Mr. Twiller, you're covering Paula up!

> MRS. RITTER. [*Trying to talk to Florence over Twiller's shoulder*] Well, he'll apologize to me, whether we've convinced him or not. [*Mrs. Fell and Hossefrosse come over to see if they can be of any assistance.*]

MRS. PAMPINELLI and TWILLER, together.

> MRS. PAMPINELLI. [*Becoming desperate*] Paula! [*Paula gives her a nervous glance.*] Will one of you go farther in! Mr. Twiller!

> TWILLER. [*Addressing Florence*] Have you convinced yourselves? [*He gives Mrs. Pampinelli an irritated look over his left shoulder.*]

FLORENCE. That there has been a mistake?

MRS. PAMPINELLI. Go farther in, one of you! [*Twiller gives her another look, then speaks to Florence.*]

TWILLER. Yes! [*Mrs. Pampinelli can contain herself no longer, so, picking up her skirt, and holding her hand against the left side of her head, she darts across the open door, to the left, and speaks to them around the edge of the door. Mrs. Fell, taking advantage of the circumstance of Mrs. Pampinelli's crossing, tiptoes up to Twiller and strikes him on the left arm, quite viciously, with the rolled manuscript. As a polite remonstrance, he shakes his left hand and foot at her. But, she is not dismayed, and repeats the attack, even more viciously. Then he turns and glares at her, and she turns away towards the right, desperately.*]

FLORENCE. A great mistake.

MRS. RITTER. Disappointed? Because, you know, we can *invent* a scandal, if you insist.

MRS. FELL. Oh, what a man! What a man!

FLORENCE and MRS. PAMPINELLI, together.

> FLORENCE. I'm afraid *my* presence here would be a bit incongruous, even for that.

> MRS. PAMPINELLI. Go farther in, Mr. Twiller, don't both of you stand wedged in the doorway that way, it looks dreadful!

TWILLER. [*Raising his right arm and resting his hand against the jamb of the door, completely cutting off Mrs. Ritter's view of Florence*] That's the rub. [*Mrs. Ritter stands on her tiptoes to try and see over his arm, but being unsuccessful in this effort, stoops a bit, and tries to look under his arm.*]

MRS. PAMPINELLI. Take your arm down, Mr. Twiller! [*Mrs. Ritter reaches up and quietly but firmly draws Twiller's arm down. Mrs. Pampinelli turns away to the left, disgusted.*] My God! I never gave any such direction as that!

FLORENCE. Be at ease, Mr. Rush; if you were not mistaken I should have known it,—and so should you; I'm not a tragic woman. Did you want to leave any message for the Doctor, Mrs. Rush?

MRS. RITTER. [*At Twiller's right*] Yes,—[*Twiller turns his head sharply and looks right into her eyes. She steps around back of him and speaks to Florence over his left shoulder.*] I wish you'd say that my husband called—[*Twiller turns and looks into her eyes again, and she steps around back of him again, to his right.*] for my bill. [*She reaches out and starts to draw the door to. Twiller, very ill at ease, and awkwardly looking from side to side, not knowing just how to get out gracefully, makes a full turn round to his right.*]

TWILLER. [*Raising his hat to Florence*] Good evening, Mrs. Arlington. [*Mrs. Ritter closes the door, causing him to drop his cane; but he's too excited to notice it.*]

HOSSEFROSSE. [*Standing at the right door, extending his hand*] Great, old man!

TWILLER. [*Dropping his gloves, as he shakes hands*] Thanks. [*He continues to the right.*]

MRS. FELL. [*As he passes below her*] Splendid, Ralph! What happened to your mustache? [*She laughs.*]

TWILLER. Can you beat that, Nelly! I couldn't *coax* that thing off before I went on!

HOSSEFROSSE. [*Holding the knob of the right door*] Shush!

MRS. FELL. I don't think the audience noticed it.

HOSSEFROSSE. [*Turning to them*] Shush! [*Twiller goes down to the right, and Mrs. Fell returns to her manuscript. The left door is flung open. They all watch eagerly.*]

MRS. RITTER. [*Inside the left door*] If you will, please?

FLORENCE. Certainly.

MRS. RITTER. Thanks.

FLORENCE. Don't mention it.

MRS. RITTER. [*Trying to appear very bold*] Good bye.

FLORENCE. Good bye. [*Mrs. Ritter gives another famous laugh, sways through the door, tripping over the door-strip, closes the door, looks at Mrs. Pampinelli, who is standing at the left, and bursts out laughing. There is prolonged applause from beyond the flats.*]

MRS. PAMPINELLI. Splendid, Paula!

HOSSEFROSSE. [*Listening intently for his cue, from beyond the flats*] Shush-shush! [*Mrs. Ritter looks at him, still laughing foolishly.*]

MRS. FELL. [*Waving at Paula*] Lovely, dear!

MRS. RITTER. [*Turning to Mrs. Pampinelli*] I forgot my umbrella.

MRS. PAMPINELLI. Where is it?

MRS. RITTER. I left it on the stage.

MRS. PAMPINELLI. That doesn't matter. [*Hossefrosse tries to silence them by dint of impatient gesturing with his right hand.*]

MRS. RITTER. Oh, Betty, I think I saw Clara Sheppard out there!

MRS. PAMPINELLI. Not really?

HOSSEFROSSE. Shush!

FLORENCE. [*From beyond the flats*] You can come out now, Clyde, they've gone. [*Hossefrosse yanks the right door open, causing the wood-wing at the right to topple and fall forward.*]

TWILLER. [*Leaping to catch it, before it hits Mrs. Fell*] Hold it! [*Mrs. Fell hunches her arms and shoulders and screams.*]

MRS. PAMPINELLI. [*Rushing over from the left*] What is it?

TWILLER. [*Struggling to set the wing up in place again*] This thing nearly fell! Just got it in time! [*Mrs. Fell moves out of the way, over to the left, and Mrs. Pampinelli tries to assist Twiller.*]

MRS. PAMPINELLI. Is it all right now?

TWILLER. [*Brushing his hands and clothes, and coming forward at the right*] Yes, it's all right now. Just got it in time.

MRS. FELL. [*Rushing up to Mrs. Ritter, who is coming towards her from the left, and shaking her by the arms*] Oh, you were marvelous, darling! [*Mrs. Ritter giggles foolishly.*] I could just hug you!

MRS. RITTER. I forgot my umbrella.

MRS. FELL. Wonderful performance! [*She steps to the right door and opens her manuscript. Mrs. Ritter moves a little to the right and stands looking at the wood-wing.*]

MRS. PAMPINELLI. [*Turning from a more precise adjustment of the wood-wing*] Oh, Mr. Twiller!

TWILLER. Yes?

MRS. PAMPINELLI. How did you and Paula get wedged in that door that way, over there a moment ago?

TWILLER. [*On Mrs. Pampinelli's right*] Oh, I'm awfully sorry about that! I got a little twisted on— [*Mrs. Ritter comes to Mrs. Pampinelli's left.*]

MRS. PAMPINELLI. [*Turning to Mrs. Ritter*] I was just asking Mr. Twiller about that business in the door.

MRS. PAMPINELLI, MRS. RITTER and TWILLER, together.

> MRS. PAMPINELLI. Of course, it really didn't matter very much.

> MRS. RITTER. Oh, my dear, wasn't that just too dreadful! But I didn't know what to do! I knew there was something wrong, but I didn't know what it was!

TWILLER. It was *my* fault. I got a little twisted there in my business-cues. I got up to the door a couple of speeches too soon.

MRS. PAMPINELLI. I don't think the audience noticed it.

MRS. FELL. [*Frantically searching in the manuscript*] Shush!

MRS. RITTER. Don't you think they did, Betty?

MRS. FELL. Shush! [*They all turn and look at her. Mrs. Pampinelli steps towards her.*]

MRS. PAMPINELLI. Is somebody up? [*Nelly simply silences her with a gesture, and opens the door slightly.*]

MRS. FELL. [*Prompting through the door*] You've all been listening to a lot of damned, cheap gossip!

HOSSEFROSSE. [*From beyond the flats*] You've all been listening to a lot of damned, cheap gossip!

FLORENCE. [*Beyond the flats*] Which should show you that people are talking.

MRS. PAMPINELLI. Somebody up? [*Nelly just shakes her head and relaxes.*] Mr. Hossefrosse?

MRS. FELL. The "damned, cheap gossip" line.

MRS. PAMPINELLI. [*Listening keenly*] Is he all right again?

MRS. FELL. Yes, he's all right now;—but it's funny how that line has sent him up at every performance.

MRS. PAMPINELLI. [*Turning to rejoin Mrs. Ritter and Twiller*] It's purely mental.

HOSSEFROSSE. [*From beyond the flats, violently*] No! [*The stage manager, over at the left, jumps to his feet, causing the hammer to fall from his pocket. The door-slam also falls, with a bang. The stage manager has been dozing, and the thunder of Mr. Hossefrosse's outburst has considerably startled him. He comes forward at the left and looks over at Mrs. Fell, to inquire the cause of the disturbance.*]

MRS. FELL. [*Motioning to him with her manuscript*] Shush! [*He looks about and then goes back and picks up the hammer and door-slam. As he resumes his seat he takes another glance around.*]

MRS. RITTER. [*As Mrs. Pampinelli comes forward again at the right, between her and Twiller*] You know, I felt like a perfect fool standing there in that door, but I couldn't catch what you were saying. [*Twiller laughs.*]

MRS. PAMPINELLI. Well, dear, I *really* don't think the audience noticed it.

TWILLER. I hope they didn't.

MRS. RITTER. It must have looked awful.

MRS. PAMPINELLI. No, dear, it didn't, really; you both covered it up very nicely.

TWILLER. I *tried* to cover it up when my mustache fell off, too;—but I had so many *lines* right in there. I held it on as long as I could, but I was afraid the audience was beginning to notice it.

MRS. PAMPINELLI. I was so glad you had the presence of mind not to attempt to stick it on again when it fell off the *second* time.

TWILLER. I was afraid to take the time. I had a cue right there; so when it fell off the second time, I just—let it lie there. [*He makes a casual gesture with his right hand.*]

MRS. PAMPINELLI. That was quite right.

TWILLER. [*Laughing a little*] It's out there yet.

MRS. RITTER. [*Giggling*] So is my umbrella. [*They all laugh.*] Oh, listen, Betty dear! I think I'll just run upstairs for a minute and use that telephone—see how Fred is. [*She starts towards the left.*]

MRS. PAMPINELLI. [*Following her*] Yes, do, Paula.

MRS. RITTER. I'm kind of worried about him.

MRS. PAMPINELLI. See if he's regained consciousness yet.

MRS. RITTER. [*Regardless of the fact that a play is in progress*] Excuse me!

MRS. FELL. [*Looking up from her manuscript*] Shush!

MRS. PAMPINELLI. Certainly, dear. [*Twiller raises his hat towards her, and she waves back at him. Then he goes up at the right and peeks through the side wings.*] Oh, Paula!

MRS. RITTER. [*Turning*] Yes, dear?

MRS. PAMPINELLI. Be sure and get down in time for the curtains.

MRS. RITTER. Oh, yes.

MRS. PAMPINELLI. I imagine there'll be a lot of flowers come over.

MRS. RITTER. [*Starting up at the left*] I'll be right down as soon as I telephone.

MRS. PAMPINELLI. Yes, do, dear. [*Mrs. Ritter goes out at the left, and Mrs. Pampinelli turns, touching her hair, and starts back towards the right. Something falls beyond the flats. She stops dead, and listens. Mrs. Fell turns quickly and peeks through the right door. Twiller comes forward at the right and looks inquiringly.*]

FLORENCE. [*Just audible beyond the flats*] Then, you've allowed him to think so.

MRS. PAMPINELLI. What's that?

FLORENCE. [*Beyond the flats*] Perhaps it is.

MRS. FELL. [*Turning to Mrs. Pampinelli, and quite casually*] He knocked the ash-tray over. [*Mrs. Pampinelli relaxes, and proceeds to arrange the beaded ornaments on her dress, while Mrs. Fell moves a bit farther over to the right and stands listening, manuscript and lorgnon in hand. Twiller crosses to the left, below Mrs. Fell, and gathers up his gloves and cane.*]

HOSSEFROSSE. [*Beyond the flats*] You are deliberately misinterpreting this situation! Yes you are! It's perfectly ridiculous that a physician cannot take a woman patient without being subjected to the whisperings of a lot of vulgar scandal-mongers.

FLORENCE. This is not a romantic age, Clyde.

TWILLER. [*Coming to Mrs. Pampinelli's right*] Was that inflection of mine any better tonight on that line, "I'm puzzled."?

MRS. PAMPINELLI. Oh, very much better, I was listening for it.

TWILLER. [*Thoughtfully*] I never seemed to get the sense of that line until tonight. It just seemed to—come to me, out there on the stage.

MRS. PAMPINELLI. Oh, that is a very significant line, Mr. Twiller, coming where it does. [*Spindler comes wandering on from the left, comes forward, looks about, and goes up to the side wing and looks through.*]

TWILLER. I felt a great deal easier in that new business of turning—down at the bookcase that you gave me last night.

MRS. PAMPINELLI. [*With a touch of smugness*] Much better.

TWILLER. Did you notice it?

MRS. PAMPINELLI. Well, of course, I couldn't see it, I was here; but I could sense it; and I could tell from the *tone* of the scene that it was better. [*Spindler moves over to the extreme left, about half-way back, and, taking the refractory telephone-bell-arrangement from his pocket, starts to tinker with it.*]

TWILLER. I just turned my head *this* way, [*He turns his head sharply to the right, keeping his body and shoulders perfectly rigid.*]

MRS. PAMPINELLI. Excellent.

TWILLER. [*Turning back to her*] Without moving my body.

MRS. PAMPINELLI. Very good.

TWILLER. Instead of making the full swing around, [*He makes a complete swing around on his right foot.*] the way I had been doing. [*Mrs. Fell raises her lorgnon and looks over, curiously.*]

MRS. PAMPINELLI. A very good change.

TWILLER. [*Very seriously*] I *felt* that it got them.

MRS. PAMPINELLI. Well, you see, it gave them the full benefit of your expression. [*They nod agreement.*]

TWILLER. There's a great deal of light and shade in that part, right in there.

MRS. PAMPINELLI. [*Deprecatingly*] Ho! my dear,—it is *all* light and shade;— even to the gestures. [*She makes a Delsartian movement with her arms and hands. Mrs. Fell comes forward a little further and observes the gesture keenly, through her lorgnon.*] ....

TWILLER. [*Rather troubled, and shaking his head a bit*] I've got to put in a lot of work on *my* gestures,—they're bad, I know.

MRS. PAMPINELLI. Well, I shouldn't exactly say that your gestures were bad; but I think, perhaps——

TWILLER. [*Leaning heavily on his cane*] I—ah—I think I try too hard to be natural.

MRS. PAMPINELLI. [*Smiling, biting her lip, and rolling her eyes*] That's exactly what I was going to say. Your gestures are, in a way, *too* natural. [*She gives a little mirthless laugh, and, out of courtesy, he joins her.*] Of course, that is a very virtuous fault; but it isn't pretty, is it? [*She laughs again.*]

TWILLER. No, it isn't. [*The stage manager gets up, stretches himself, and comes forward at the left.*]

MRS. PAMPINELLI. And, after all, the function of art is to be pretty, is it not? [*She repeats the floating gesture.*]

TWILLER. [*Trying to imitate her*] I don't seem to be able—to *do* that, the way you do. [*Mrs. Fell feels the call, and, putting the manuscript under her arm, tries rather unsuccessfully to copy the movement.*]

MRS. PAMPINELLI. Oh, it is purely a matter of experience, Mr. Twiller. But when you've been in the work as long as I have,—you'll realize that the bird's-wing gesture is the *only* gesture. [*She illustrates again, for the edification of her disciples; and they attempt rather faithfully to imitate her. The stage manager stands looking at them.*]

FLORENCE. [*Beyond the flats*] But it has its compensations—You'll have your memories, [*There is a confusion of voices from beyond the flats, and cries of "Sit down!"*]

MRS. PAMPINELLI. [*Startled*] What's that? [*Mrs. Fell rushes to the right door and peeks through, Twiller goes over to the right and up, and the stage manager rushes back to his post and disappears at the left.*] What is it, Nelly?

MRS. FELL. [*Turning suddenly to Mrs. Pampinelli*] They're carrying a man out of the audience! [*She looks back again through the peek, and Mrs. Pampinelli steps to the left door and peeks. Mrs. Sheppard sweeps on up at the left, and comes forward. She is a slim brunette, in her thirties, very attractive, and wearing the very last whisper in widow's weeds. She looks around, rather dramatically, then sees the ladies. Mrs. Fell looks away from the peek-hole and sees her.*] Betty, there's Clara!

MRS. PAMPINELLI. [*Looking at Nelly*] What?

MRS. FELL. [*Not wishing to be heard*] Clara Sheppard. [*Mrs. Pampinelli turns quickly.*]

MRS. PAMPINELLI. Oh, Clara! [*She goes towards her, and Clara advances a little.*] I'm so glad to see you! [*Clara breaks down and weeps.*] Now, don't do that, dear. You know Jimmy wouldn't for anything in the world want you to feel that way. So be brave, honey. It was splendid of you to come here at all. And you look wonderful.

MRS. SHEPPARD. I must look perfectly dreadful.

MRS. PAMPINELLI. You don't look anything of the kind, darling, you look perfectly beautiful.

MRS. SHEPPARD. All I've done is cry.

MRS. PAMPINELLI. I know just how you feel.

MRS. SHEPPARD. But I didn't want you to think I'd entirely forsaken the cause.

MRS. PAMPINELLI. Oh, my dear, we understood perfectly.

MRS. SHEPPARD. But I just felt I *had* to come here tonight.

MRS. PAMPINELLI. Have you been out in front, Clara?

MRS. SHEPPARD. Yes, I just *had* to see it. I don't think anybody saw me; I came in late, and stood way at the back.

MRS. PAMPINELLI. They'd hardly see you.

MRS. SHEPPARD. I don't think so; I kept my veil lowered. Of course, I should *love* to have been right down in front, where I could get all those *wonderful* little subtleties. But, you know how it is,—I was afraid people might not understand my being here at all. It's only three weeks, you know.

MRS. PAMPINELLI. They wouldn't, either.

MRS. SHEPPARD. That's what I thought.

MRS. PAMPINELLI. I don't suppose there's one person in *ten thousand* that has dramatic instinct enough to appreciate the way you feel. [*She turns to the left door and listens.*]

MRS. SHEPPARD. [*Beginning to cry again*] The flowers in the lobby are perfectly beautiful.

MRS. PAMPINELLI. [*Still listening*] Yes, but I'm not having them passed over the footlights tonight.

MRS. SHEPPARD. [*Drying her eyes*] No?

MRS. PAMPINELLI. Except one bouquet for each of the ladies. It took up too much time the last time.

MRS. SHEPPARD. [*Glancing about*] Where's Paula?

MRS. PAMPINELLI. She's upstairs, telephoning. She's rather annoyed about Fred, you know.

MRS. SHEPPARD. What about him? [*Mrs. Pampinelli turns from the door suddenly and looks at her.*]

FLORENCE. [*Beyond the flats*] There is, my dear boy,—for lots of people——

MRS. PAMPINELLI. Why, my dear, didn't you hear?—about him falling downstairs last night?

MRS. SHEPPARD. Oh, not really!

MRS. PAMPINELLI. [*Coming towards her*] He fell almost the entire flight.

MRS. SHEPPARD. Oh, dear me!

MRS. PAMPINELLI. Poor Paula's terribly upset.

MRS. SHEPPARD. What was he doing, coming down the stairs?

MRS. PAMPINELLI. No, he was watching our rehearsal. You know, we held the final rehearsal at Paula's house last night—we couldn't get this place.

MRS. SHEPPARD. [*Solicitously*] Well, did he break any *bones*, Betty?

MRS. PAMPINELLI. No,—Doctor Wentworth said—he was unconscious before he hit the floor. He said the fall was the result of a collapse; and that he would have fallen no matter where he had been. Unfortunately, he just happened to be on the stairs. [*She turns back again to the left door.*]

MRS. SHEPPARD. [*Retrospectively*] I *thought* he looked pale when I saw him out there tonight. [*Mrs. Pampinelli turns suddenly and looks at her.*]

FLORENCE. [*Beyond the flats*] And you have a very modern wife.

MRS. PAMPINELLI. When you saw him out here, you mean? [*She indicates the audience beyond the flats.*]

MRS. SHEPPARD. Yes; he was standing out there at the back, right near *me*.

MRS. PAMPINELLI. [*Coming towards her again*] You *must* be mistaken, Clara.

MRS. SHEPPARD. No, Betty, I'm quite *sure* I saw him.

MRS. PAMPINELLI. Well, the only thing *I* know is that Paula said he hadn't regained consciousness when she left the house this evening at seven-thirty. [*Mrs. Ritter comes on up at the back, from the left, and comes forward.*] Here's Paula now!

MRS. SHEPPARD. [*Turning round to her left*] Poor dear, she must be terribly upset.

MRS. RITTER. [*Extending her arms*] Clara, dear! [*Mrs. Sheppard bursts into tears again.*] This is so nice of you! [*They embrace each other, and Mrs. Ritter starts to cry.*]

MRS. PAMPINELLI. Isn't she the sweet thing! [*The door at the right opens.*]

MRS. FELL. [*To the ladies*] Shush! [*They all turn and look toward the right door.*]

MRS. PAMPINELLI. [*With a gesture to Mrs. Ritter and Mrs. Sheppard*] Shush! [*Hossefrosse comes out the right door.*]

FLORENCE. [*Beyond the flats*] It's gotten very chilly.

HOSSEFROSSE. [*Picking up his hat, cane and gloves from the chair*] Yes, I know it has; I just came in a few minutes ago.

FLORENCE. You had tickets for the theatre, didn't you?

HOSSEFROSSE. [*Stepping back through the right door again*] Yes.

FLORENCE. Why not take me?—for a change. [*The door closes.*] You used to— years ago.

MRS. PAMPINELLI. [*Turning to Mrs. Ritter and Mrs. Sheppard*] Paula, Clara says she thinks she saw Mr. Ritter out there tonight.

MRS. RITTER. [*Standing at the left*] My dear, Jenny just told me over the telephone that he regained consciousness a half-hour after I left the house, and went out. Said she thought from the way he talked he was coming here.

MRS. SHEPPARD. [*In the center*] Yes, I was *sure* I saw him standing out there— [*Turning to Mrs. Ritter*] I was just telling Betty.

MRS. RITTER. I wonder if he's out there yet.

MRS. SHEPPARD. I don't know, dear.

MRS. PAMPINELLI. How much of the play did you see, Clara?

MRS. SHEPPARD. Why, I stayed just as long as I could, Betty. But when Paula came on, and I heard those lines of mine again, I just couldn't stand it. [*She breaks down, and buries her face in her handkerchief.*]

MRS. PAMPINELLI. [*Laying her hand on her arm*] I know, Clara—you're such an artist.

MRS. SHEPPARD. [*Pressing her hands against her bosom*] Everything just seemed to come back on me.

MRS. PAMPINELLI. I know how it is, dear.

MRS. SHEPPARD. [*Speaking directly to Mrs. Pampinelli*] I got thinking how Jimmy would feel, if he could know, that *he* was the cause of standing in the way of my first *real* opportunity. [*She cries again.*]

MRS. PAMPINELLI. [*Raising her eyes to Heaven*] Perhaps he does know, dear.

MRS. SHEPPARD. [*Turning to her again*] I mean, you know, he was always so anxious about my getting into the work. And, somehow or other, I always *felt*—that I could have done so much with that part. [*Mrs. Ritter gives a vague little laugh, and Mrs. Sheppard turns to her quickly.*] Oh, of course, you were perfectly *adorable* in it, darling, I don't mean that— [*The left door opens, and Florence is standing in it, about to come out.*]

MRS. FELL. [*To Mrs. Pampinelli, Mrs. Ritter and Mrs. Sheppard*] Shush!

MRS. PAMPINELLI. [*Turning and going closer to the left door*] Excuse me, Clara.

MRS. SHEPPARD. Certainly, dear. [*Twiller comes forward at the right.*]

FLORENCE. [*Stepping through the door*] By the way, there was a Mr. Robinson telephoned this morning, after you'd left the house— [*Mrs. Sheppard waves her handkerchief at Florence, and Florence replies by quietly flicking her fingers at her. Then, still keeping in her character, she moves slowly towards the right, leaving the door open behind her.*] He said something about a list being correct.

HOSSEFROSSE. [*Appearing in the doorway, carrying his hat, cane and gloves*] Yes, I know. [*He reaches towards the left, beyond the flats, as though he were pushing an electric-light button, then thrusts his head through the door and says in a fierce whisper.*] Lights.

FLORENCE. Lights out!

MRS. FELL and MRS. PAMPINELLI, together.

    MRS. FELL. Put out the lights, somebody!

MRS. PAMPINELLI. Lights, Mr. Stage Manager! [*The stage manager appears from the left, at the back.*]

SPINDLER. [*Springing from the left, where he has been engaged in trying to repair the telephone-battery*] Lights out!

MRS. PAMPINELLI. Where are you! [*The stage manager reaches up and pulls one of the switches on the switch-board at the back, and the lights beyond the flats go out; then he disappears again at the left.*]

SPINDLER and HOSSEFROSSE, together.

> SPINDLER. I was right here!

> HOSSEFROSSE. [*Coming through the door*] Yes, I know,— [*Closing the door behind him*] I talked to him. [*Puts his hat on*]

MRS. PAMPINELLI. Well, why aren't you right *here*, where you should be! Stand by for the curtain, now,—see if you can do that much right. Surely, it's the old story of the lark,—if you want a thing done, do it yourself! Curtain!

SPINDLER. [*Shouting*] Curtain! [*The curtain, beyond the flats, begins to roll down, and there is thunderous applause.*]

MRS. FELL. [*To Florence*] Marvelous, darling! [*Florence waves at her, turns, and rushes back towards the left.*] Just lovely, Huxley!

HOSSEFROSSE. Thanks. [*He turns to the left.*]

MRS. PAMPINELLI. Lights up! Splendid, children!

FLORENCE. I'm awfully glad to see you, Clara!

MRS. SHEPPARD, MRS. PAMPINELLI, HOSSEFROSSE and SPINDLER, together.

> MRS. SHEPPARD. [*Shaking hands with Florence*] You were wonderful, Flossie!

> MRS. PAMPINELLI. Take up the curtain, Mr. Stage Manager!

> HOSSEFROSSE. Thank you very much.

> SPINDLER. Lights up! [*The stage manager appears from the left and pulls the switch again, and the lights beyond the flats go on.*]

SPINDLER. Take it up! [*The stage manager darts off again to the left. The waltz-music on the piano, beyond the flats, begins again.*]

HOSSEFROSSE. [*Lifting his hat and beaming*] Hello, Clara!

MRS. SHEPPARD. Wonderful! [*He deprecates profusely. The curtain rises again.*]

MRS. PAMPINELLI. Go on, Mr. Hossefrosse! [*He opens the right door, removing his hat.*] Wait a moment, Mr. Hossefrosse! Come on, Florence! [*Hossefrosse stops uncertainly in the doorway and looks at Mrs. Pampinelli.*] It's all right! Go on! [*She opens the left door.*] Here, go on here, Florence! [*They go on, bowing, and there is prolonged applause.*] Come on, Paula! go on here! [*The curtain descends again. Paula scurries to the left door, giggling.*] Where's Mr. Twiller!

TWILLER. [*Springing over from the right, where he has been talking and laughing with Mrs. Fell*] Here I am!

MRS. PAMPINELLI. [*Turning to the left*] Take it up again, Mr. Stage Manager! [*Turning back to Twiller, and opening the door*] Here, Mr. Twiller, take Paula on! [*The curtain can be seen through the left door rising again.*] Come on, Paula! [*Twiller drops his cane, in shifting it from his right hand to his left.*] Hurry up! [*He snatches the cane up, and, taking Paula by the arm, escorts her through the door. But she trips over the door-strip, nevertheless. And there is sustained applause. Mrs. Fell, over at the right, begins to preen herself feverishly. Mrs. Pampinelli closes the door slowly, and stands listening, smiling. Teddy appears up at the left and comes forward, pressing his violet handkerchief to his brow, and looking very wan. Mrs. Pampinelli turns to him.*] Come on, Teddy, hurry up! They're just going on! How do you feel? [*The curtain descends.*]

TEDDY. Only fair.

MRS. PAMPINELLI. [*Taking him by the right arm and urging him towards the right*] Here, Nelly, go on for a bow with Teddy! [*Rushing back towards the left*] Take it up again, Mr. Stage Manager!

MRS. PAMPINELLI, TEDDY and SPINDLER, together.

MRS. PAMPINELLI. Mr. Spindler!

TEDDY. [*Opening the right door*] Come on, Nelly!

SPINDLER. [*Half-way back, at the left*] Take it up! [*Rushing forward at the left*] Yes?

MRS. PAMPINELLI and MRS. FELL, together.

MRS. PAMPINELLI. [*To Spindler*] Keep it going up and down till I tell you to stop! And keep it up the next time till the gentlemen get the flowers!

MRS. FELL. [*Shrinking away a little more to the right of the door, but still preening herself, almost hysterically, and breaking into a little nervous laugh*] Oh, no, really, dear! I wouldn't *think* of it! [*Teddy goes through the right door. The curtain can be seen rising again; then the door closes after him; and Mrs. Fell continues talking, to herself.*] Why, what have I done that I should go on. I wouldn't mind if I'd taken some part in the play,—but I certainly don't see—

MRS. PAMPINELLI. [*Rushing back to the right*] Go on, Nelly! what are you waiting for? [*The curtain descends again. Mrs. Fell rushes towards Mrs. Pampinelli.*]

MRS. FELL. [*Handing Mrs. Pampinelli the rolled manuscript*] Hold this!

MRS. PAMPINELLI. Hurry, dear! [*Mrs. Fell rushes to the right door, settles herself finally, and flings the door open. The curtain is just rising. And, placing one hand upon her bosom, dropping her eyes and smiling, Nelly sways through the door, acknowledging the plaudits. Mrs. Pampinelli, standing in the middle of the stage, applauds, also, hitting the manuscript against her hand. The door closes after Mrs. Fell. Mrs. Sheppard, over at the left, suddenly bursts into tears and buries her face in her handkerchief. Mrs. Pampinelli turns quickly and looks at her, then crosses towards her.*] Do you want to take a bow, Clara?

MRS. SHEPPARD. Oh, no, thank you! [*Mrs. Pampinelli turns back to the left door.*]

MRS. PAMPINELLI. Get those flowers, boys! Keep it up, Mr. Stage Manager! Come on, Clara! go on for a bow! [*Reaches for Mrs. Sheppard's hand*]

MRS. SHEPPARD. [*Giving Mrs. Pampinelli her hand, and allowing herself to be drawn towards the right*] Do you think they'd understand, Betty?

MRS. PAMPINELLI. Of course, they would, my dear! They know it isn't your fault that you're not appearing! [*Mrs. Fell thrusts open the right door. She has a basket of roses in her hand.*]

MRS. FELL. They're *calling* for you, Betty! [*Someone in the audience can be heard calling Mrs. Pampinelli's name.*]

MRS. PAMPINELLI. Here, Nelly, take Clara on for a bow!

MRS. FELL. [*Impatiently*] They're calling for you, dear! [*Mrs. Sheppard hastily throws her veil back, dramatically.*]

MRS. PAMPINELLI. I'll take one alone, afterwards! [*The applause swells again.*] Go on, Clara!

MRS. FELL. [*Extending her right hand*] Come on, dear!

MRS. SHEPPARD. [*Giving Mrs. Fell her left hand*] Oh, I don't feel that I should! [*Mrs. Fell keeps the door open, and Clara droops through, bowing. Then Mrs. Fell closes the door and Mrs. Pampinelli turns to the left.*]

MRS. PAMPINELLI. Keep it up, Mr. Spindler!

SPINDLER. Keep it up!

HOSSEFROSSE. [*Thrusting open the left door*] Mrs. Pampinelli! [*There is a vision through the door of the various artists bowing towards the back wall, all the ladies laden with flowers.*]

MRS. PAMPINELLI. All right, dear! I'm coming! [*Hossefrosse closes the door, and Mrs. Pampinelli deftly touches her hair and flings her train out to its full length behind her. Then she speaks in a loud voice, so that she may be heard by those on the other side of the flats.*] Everybody stand to one side! Stand to one side, everybody! [*She pulls open the left door and stands, smiling: then she steps through the door; and, instantly, the curtain falls with a deafening crash. The door closes after her. Nelly Fell gives a piercing scream. Spindler comes rushing down from the left to the left door.*]

TEDDY. [*Shouting, beyond the flats*] Curtain!

HOSSEFROSSE. Take up the curtain!

TWILLER. Take it up! [*There is a babel of voices beyond the flats. Then the left door is thrust violently open, and Mrs. Pampinelli looks out.*]

MRS. PAMPINELLI. [*Harshly, to Spindler*] What's the matter with the curtain?

SPINDLER. [*In a panic of excitement*] Something's broke! [*The stage manager rushes on from the left and comes forward.*]

MRS. PAMPINELLI. [*Coming out through the door and calling to the stage manager, whom she hasn't seen yet*] Take up the curtain, Mr. Stage Manager!

STAGE MANAGER. I can't take it up, the guy-rope's broken! [*He goes up at the left.*]

MRS. PAMPINELLI. What? [*Mrs. Fell comes running through the right door, carrying her basket of flowers, and crosses towards the left.*]

MRS. FELL and SPINDLER, together.

> MRS. FELL. What is it, Betty?
>
> SPINDLER. [*To Mrs. Pampinelli*] He says the guy-rope's broken!

MRS. PAMPINELLI. [*Brushing him aside, to the left, and rushing up at the left*] My God! did anyone ever hear of such stupidity!

MRS. PAMPINELLI, MRS. FELL and SPINDLER, together.

> MRS. PAMPINELLI. I'll go on at the side here!
>
> MRS. FELL. What's the matter, Mr. Spindler?
>
> SPINDLER. [*Shouting after Mrs. Pampinelli*] He says he can't get it up! [*Mrs. Sheppard comes through the right doorway with an armload of American Beauty roses, and stands looking anxiously from*

- 98 -

side to side. Teddy follows her out and stands at her right, discussing the incident. Florence opens the left door and comes out. Her arms are full of tiger-lilies. She moves to the right and speaks to Mrs. Sheppard, nervously.]

STAGE MANAGER. You can't get through there, lady! [*Twiller comes out the left door.*]

MRS. PAMPINELLI and STAGE MANAGER, together;

> MRS. PAMPINELLI. I must get through somewhere!

> STAGE MANAGER. That tormentor's too narrow there!

MRS. PAMPINELLI, STAGE MANAGER and MRS. FELL, together.

> MRS. PAMPINELLI. [*Turning frantically and rushing forward again at the left*] I'll try the other side! He says it's too narrow there!

> STAGE MANAGER. I don't know how you're going to do it!

> MRS. FELL. [*As Mrs. Pampinelli sweeps between her and Spindler*] What is it he says is broken, Betty? [*Mrs. Pampinelli rushes over towards the right. She literally sweeps Twiller, who is in her path, out of the way, and he falls backward over a stage-brace, onto the floor. Mrs. Fell picks up her dress and runs after Mrs. Pampinelli.*]

SPINDLER. [*Outrunning Mrs. Fell*] The guy-rope!

MRS. FELL. Well, why doesn't he fix it! Betty! Betty dear! [*Mrs. Pampinelli rushes up at the extreme right and tries desperately to find a way of getting through; but everything is solidly masked. Hossefrosse comes out the left door, and the stage manager comes forward at the left and stands looking after Mrs. Pampinelli.*]

HOSSEFROSSE. What's the matter, can't Mrs. Pampinelli get her bow?

STAGE MANAGER. She can't get on any more from that side than she can from this! [*Hossefrosse steps out through the door and looks toward the right. The door closes after him.*] There's the same opening over there as there is here! [*The applause beyond the flats, which has kept up throughout the debacle, begins to die. Mrs. Pampinelli comes sweeping back from the right with fire in her eye,—Nelly Fell and Spindler still at her heels. She plants herself in the middle of the stage and glares at the stage manager.*]

MRS. PAMPINELLI. [*In a voice shrill with anger*] My God! what's the matter with your curtain!

STAGE MANAGER. [*Losing his temper*] The guy-rope's broken! I've told you that about a dozen times! [*He turns doggedly away to the left, as though he were going up to his chair; but he stops short and finishes his remarks to her over his left shoulder.*]

What do you want me to do, write you a letter! [*The left door is pushed quietly open; and Mrs. Ritter, with her face just visible above a perfect screen of roses, looks blankly at the stage manager.*]

MRS. RITTER. [*Vaguely*] There's something the matter with the curtain. [*The real stage curtain commences to descend.*]

STAGE MANAGER. [*Leaning towards her, assuming her general manner and tone, and flipping his hand at her*] Y-E-E-S! [*He goes up towards his chair, and Mrs. Ritter stands in wide-eyed astonishment.*]

END OF THE ACT.

THE TORCH-BEARERS.
ACT III.

NOTE:

The setting for Act III is the same as for Act I except that the small chair which Jenny brings on at the opening of the play is eliminated.

Jenny is seated at the table below the piano, reading the Pictorial Review. The door closes out at the right. She stops reading and listens. Then resumes. Ritter wanders in from the right hallway, wearing a black overcoat and a derby. The derby is a bit over one eye and his cigar is at a comic angle. Jenny sees him and rises immediately, circling around to the left to the middle of the room.

JENNY. Oh, Mr. Ritter! [*He comes into the center-door and stands there, looking at nothing.*] I didn't hear you come in, sir. Is the show over?

RITTER. [*Removing his gloves*] It's all over town by this time.

JENNY. [*Standing slightly left of the center of the room, facing him*] Mrs. Ritter just telephoned a minute ago.

RITTER. Is she alive?

JENNY. Alive, Mr. Ritter?

RITTER. [*Moving down to the table below the piano, and thrusting his gloves into his overcoat pocket*] Because if she is, she's got a charmed life. [*Commencing to unfasten his coat*] The Seamen's Institute! God help them on a night like this.

JENNY. She was anxious to know if you were still unconscious.

RITTER. [*Taking off his overcoat*] If she telephones again, tell her yes. [*He is in a tuxedo-suit.*]

JENNY. [*Crossing to him and helping him with the coat*] Ain't you feelin' well again, Mr. Ritter?

RITTER. No, Jenny, I'm not. [*He hands her his derby.*]

JENNY. [*Taking the hat and coat to the partition-seat above the piano*] Well, I'm sure I'm sorry, sir.

RITTER. [*Removing his scarf*] And after that exhibition tonight,—I don't think I ever shall feel exactly well again.

JENNY. [*Coming down at his left and passing back of him*] Was it a sad play?

RITTER. [*Handing her his scarf, and speaking with measured conviction*] The saddest thing I've ever seen in my life.

JENNY. I allus cry when a show is sad.

RITTER. Is that so?

JENNY. Yes, sir; and a funny thing about me is—the sadder it is the more I cry.

RITTER. You'd have had a big night if you'd been with me. [*She passes back of him with the scarf, to put it with the other things.*] You'd better leave those things here, Jenny, I may leave town again tonight.

JENNY. I'll leave them right here. [*She turns from an arrangement of the things and comes forward to the middle of the room.*] Did they clap much when Mrs. Ritter finished?

RITTER. [*Still standing above the table near the piano, clipping the tip of a cigar which he has taken from his pocket*] I didn't wait for the finish; they carried me out.

JENNY. I'm dyin' till she gets home, for I know exactly how she felt. [*He looks at her keenly—she is looking straight ahead.*]

RITTER. Have you been on the stage, too, Jenny?

JENNY. [*Turning to him*] No, sir, I haven't, Mr. Ritter, not lately. But when I was at home in England I used to go on every once in a while. For a bit of a change, you know.

RITTER. Yes, I know.

JENNY. We had a little club in the town I lived in, and we used to give a show twice a year. [*Ritter nods slowly and comprehendingly.*] I always took off the comical parts.

RITTER. How is it they didn't get you into this show tonight?

JENNY. Oh, I haven't been on for a long time now, Mr. Ritter. My husband put a stop to it. [*She looks away off.*]

RITTER. [*Turning to her*] What was the matter?

JENNY. [*Turning to him, suddenly*] He died.

RITTER. [*Replacing his penknife*] I see.

JENNY. And I never felt much like cuttin' up after that. [*The telephone-bell rings. She turns quickly and starts for the center-door.*]

RITTER. [*Moving over towards the mantelpiece*] See who that is, Jenny.

JENNY. [*Hurrying out into the left hallway*] Yes, sir.

RITTER. [*Getting a match from the table below the mantelpiece*] Anybody for me, I've gone into permanent retirement.

JENNY. [*At the telephone*] Yes? [*He listens narrowly.*] Mr. Ritta? [*He makes a rapid movement towards her.*] Oh, Mrs. Ritta?

RITTER. [*In a subdued tone*] Who do they want?

JENNY. [*Into the telephone*] No, mam, she hasn't got home yet. [*Lowering the telephone and speaking to Ritter*] Mrs. Ritter.

RITTER. [*Casually*] Who is it, the police? [*He lights his cigar.*]

JENNY. [*Into the telephone*] All right, Mrs. Livingston, I'll give her your message as soon as she comes in. You're more than welcome I'm sure. [*She hangs up and comes to the center-door.*]

RITTER. [*Looking at her*] Mrs. Livingston?

JENNY. Yes, sir.

RITTER. What did she want?

JENNY. She sez she wanted to congratulate Mrs. Ritter on her perfect performance tonight.

RITTER. Did she see the show?

JENNY. She didn't say, sir.

RITTER. [*Conclusively, and crossing in front of her down to the window at the right*] She didn't see it. If any of those women come back here with Mrs. Ritter, Jenny,—say that I'm not home yet, do you understand.

JENNY. [*Settling the overcoat on the partition-seat*] Yes, sir.

RITTER. [*Looking through the window*] And that you haven't seen anything *of* me.

JENNY. Yes, sir, Mr. Ritter, all right.

RITTER. If my wife's alone, let me know as soon as she comes in.

JENNY. Yes, sir, I will. [*The telephone-bell rings, and she hurries out to answer it.*]

RITTER. [*Half turning from the window*] You haven't seen anything of me, remember.

JENNY. No, sir. [*Into the telephone*] Yes, sir? [*He listens, without turning.*] No, sir, she hasn't got home yet. [*She lowers the telephone and looks at him, wide-eyed. He feels that she's looking at him and turns suddenly.*]

RITTER. [*Taking a step towards her, below the piano*] What is it?

JENNY. [*Into the telephone*] No, sir, he hasn't got home yet neither.

RITTER. [*Apprehensively*] Do they want me? [*She nods yes.*] Who is it? [*She nods that she doesn't know.*] Police Headquarters I'll bet a ten dollar note! [*He crosses down below the table at the left and around up to the mantelpiece.] Tell them that I had absolutely nothing to do with her going on! That I didn't hear about it until last night! [*He crosses back again down towards the table below the piano.*] And that I've been unconscious ever since.

JENNY. [*Into the telephone*] The Times?

RITTER. [*Stopping above the table*] My God, the newspapers have got hold of it!

JENNY. [*Into the telephone*] Well, just a minute, please.

RITTER. [*Turning suddenly to her*] Tell them she did it on a bet!

JENNY. The Times newspaper wants to know if Mrs. Ritter has a full-length photograph of herself for the morning paper.

RITTER. [*Emphatically, and going out through the center-door into the right hallway and up the stairs*] Tell them NO!

JENNY. [*Into the telephone*] Hello.

RITTER. But that she'll have some taken as soon as she gets out of jail. [*He goes through the arched doorway at the head of the stairs.*]

JENNY. [*Into the telephone*] Why, I couldn't say, sir, whether Mrs. Ritter has a photograph of herself or not, sir; but I'll give her your message as soon as she comes in.

MRS. PAMPINELLI. [*In the right hallway*] Hurry, Theodore.

JENNY. [*Still at the telephone*] You're more than welcome I'm sure. [*She hangs up and hurries in through the center-door, glancing out the right hallway as she comes and, gathering up Mr. Ritter's overcoat, derby and scarf, hurries over above the table at the left and out.*]

MRS. PAMPINELLI. [*In the right hallway*] Be careful of those jonquils. Now, be careful, Theodore! Now go back and fetch the others. [*Coming into view, and seeing Jenny coming in again at the left door*] Oh, you're up, Jenny, aren't you! [*She comes through the center-door, carrying her fan and an armload of orchids and red chrysanthemums, and wearing an enormous flowing cape of ruffled black lace, touched all over with tiny circular sequins in gold. Her dress, of course, is the ruby-velvet one of the preceding act.*]

JENNY. Yes, mam, I'm up.

MRS. PAMPINELLI. [*Hastening to the table below the piano*] I'm so glad; I hope I haven't roused you. [*She puts her fan on the piano and sets all the flowers down on the table.*] Will you go out and get those flowers from my chauffeur, Jenny?

JENNY. [*Going out through the center-door into the right hallway*] Yes, mam.

MRS. PAMPINELLI. [*Arranging the flowers on the table*] He's set them right down there in the hallway. I came right on in when I found the door unlocked; I was afraid you'd be asleep.

JENNY. No, mam, I was waitin' up.

MRS. PAMPINELLI. [*Sweeping around to her left and up to the center-door*] Well, that's perfectly angelic of you I'm sure. [*She stands on the left side of the center-door and looks out into the right hallway.*] Can you manage, dear?

JENNY. [*Appearing from the right*] I think so. [*She struggles through the center-door carrying an enormous horseshoe, made of red and white carnations and ferns. It is at least four feet high, set upon an easel, and across the front of it is a strip of white-satin ribbon ten inches wide with the word "SUCCESS" inscribed upon it in blue-velvet letters. She is also carrying a huge basket of jonquils, and a star made of white pansies. This last touch is fastened upon a violet easel.*]

MRS. PAMPINELLI. Let me help you, child. [*She takes the basket of jonquils and the star of pansies from Jenny.*] Now, set that right down there. [*She indicates a point in front of the mantelpiece for the horseshoe, and Jenny crosses in front of her with it.*] I want Mrs. Ritter to see it *first*, when she comes in,—it's so appropriate. [*She sets the basket of jonquils on the piano.*] I suppose we can put these down anywhere here until she comes, can't we? [*She sets the easel of pansies down on the floor at the right of the table below the piano.*]

JENNY. [*Having set the horseshoe down in front of the mantelpiece*] This way, Mrs. Pampinelli?

MRS. PAMPINELLI. No, dear, *facing* the door.

JENNY. Oh, I see. [*She turns it round facing the center-door.*]

MRS. PAMPINELLI. That's it. I want it to catch her eye as she comes in. And now will you go back and fetch the others, Jenny?

JENNY. [*Hurrying out through the center-door*] Yes, mam.

MRS. PAMPINELLI. [*Gathering up the chrysanthemums from the table*] And these chrysanthemums, [*She sweeps across towards the mantelpiece and turns to her left, strewing the chrysanthemums through the center-door and down toward the table at the left.*] I'll just strew in her pathway. [*Jenny comes in from the right hallway carrying a huge anchor of vivid red roses, with a broad band of navy-blue ribbon running diagonally across it, and the words "SEAMEN'S INSTITUTE" in white-velvet letters. She stands right in the center-door, holding it, waiting for instructions as to its disposition from Mrs. Pampinelli. But Mrs. Pampinelli is lost in admiration of it, standing just to the left of the center-door.*] Now, set that right down here, Jenny. [*She indicates a point at the extreme left, below the door, and Jenny hastens to place it there, setting it down half-facing the center-door; and Mrs. Pampinelli stands up at the center-door admiring it.*]

Hope! [*Jenny turns to her and gives a faint little laugh.*] Hope, for the success [*She indicates the horseshoe with a gesture.*] of our enterprise. [*They both laugh, and Mrs. Pampinelli steps quickly down to the table below the piano and picks up the orchids.*] And these orchids, I think I shall just put right here on this table. [*She crosses to the table below the casement-window and puts them down; then straightens up and sighs.*] Ho, dear me, I'm warm! [*She crosses back between the piano and the table below it, picking up her fan as she goes.*]

JENNY. [*Moving up and across back of the table at the left, towards the center of the room*] 'Tis a bit warm.

MRS. PAMPINELLI. [*Fanning herself, as she moves towards the middle of the room*] And then I hurried so,—foolishly.

JENNY. Did everything go along all right?

MRS. PAMPINELLI. Magnificently, my dear child! And Mrs. Ritter was a positive sensation.

JENNY. Did she get all these flowers?

MRS. PAMPINELLI. [*Deprecatingly*] Ho! This isn't the half of them! We sent three automobiles full to the various hospitals. And Mrs. Fell's car was still taking them when I left. [*Jenny shakes her head from side to side in wonderment.*] These are just a few that we rescued for Mrs. Ritter. [*She moves towards the center-door.*] Sort of a little surprise for her, you know, when she gets home. [*She stands looking out into the right hallway, expectantly.*]

JENNY. They're certainly 'andsome.

MRS. PAMPINELLI. She doesn't even know that I've brought them.

JENNY. Is she comin' right home, do you know, Mrs. Pampinelli?

MRS. PAMPINELLI. [*Turning to Jenny*] Why, I *expect* her, yes. I was afraid she'd get here ahead of me. She was waiting for Mr. Ritter. [*Coming forward a little*] We heard at the hall that he was there, and she thought probably he'd come back and pick her up. He hasn't *come* home, has he?

JENNY. No, mam, I haven't seen anything of him.

MRS. PAMPINELLI. [*Laughing a little, indulgently, securing a hair-pin, and moving over towards the right*] Poor man! His wife's success has very likely gone to his head. [*She glances out the window.*]

JENNY. He went out of here about eight o'clock.

MRS. PAMPINELLI. [*Turning and coming back towards Jenny*] Yes, we were so surprised to hear that he was there at all. Because Mrs. Ritter had said that he hadn't regained consciousness up to the time she left the house.

JENNY. He hadn't, neither. I thought I 'ad two 'eads on me when I came in and saw him puttin' on 'is 'at and coat.

MRS. PAMPINELLI. Well, did he seem all right?

JENNY. Yes, he seemed right enough; but he was awful pale-lookin'. And a couple a times I spoke to 'im, he gave me kind of a funny answer. So I got a bit frightened, you know; and I asked 'im if he knew where he was goin'. And he said, "Yes," that he was goin' to see "The Torch-Bearers." Kind a flightly, you know.

MRS. PAMPINELLI. Well, he would be, naturally.

JENNY. So then,—when he got to the door, he turned around—and he sez to me—"Jenny!—if you never see me again,—I want you to know I *died* in the cause of Art."—And he went out.

MRS. PAMPINELLI. He was probably rambling a bit.

JENNY. But, he walked straight enough.

MRS. PAMPINELLI. [*Turning suddenly to the center-door*] I think I hear a machine, Jenny.

JENNY. [*Stepping across quickly below the table to the casement-window*] I'll see.

MRS. PAMPINELLI. Do quickly, dear.

JENNY. Is Mrs. Fell comin' back tonight?

MRS. PAMPINELLI. [*Looking out eagerly into the right hallway*] Yes, she's bringing the rest of the flowers. I've sent my car back for her.

JENNY. [*Turning abruptly from the window and hurrying across below the piano towards the center-door*] Here's Mrs. Ritta now!

MRS. PAMPINELLI. Is Mr. Ritter with her? [*Intercepting Jenny*] No, don't go out, Jenny! I want to hear what they say when they see the flowers. [*Turning her round by the shoulder and indicating the door down at the left*] You go into the other room there, and I'll hide here— [*She moves forward at the right and across below the piano.*] in this window.

JENNY. [*Hurrying towards the door at the left*] All right, mam.

MRS. PAMPINELLI. [*Stopping near the window and turning to Jenny*] And, Jenny dear!

JENNY. [*Turning at the left door*] Yes, mam?

MRS. PAMPINELLI. Don't come out—until you hear *me* say "SURPRISE!"

JENNY. All right, Mrs. Pampinelli, I won't. [*Mrs. Pampinelli steps into the alcove of the window, then turns again to Jenny.*]

MRS. PAMPINELLI. Now, remember, Jenny,—"SURPRISE!"

JENNY. Yes, I know. [*She closes the door, and Mrs. Pampinelli conceals herself behind the window-drapery. There is a slight pause; then Mrs. Ritter hurries in from the right hallway, carrying a marvelous bouquet of American Beauty roses. She comes in through the center-door and stands, looking, with a touch of astonishment, at the horseshoe. Then her eyes wander down to the anchor; and then over to the easel at the right. She is gowned in a very pale shade of gray lace, with gray-silk slippers and stockings; and around her head she is wearing a wreath of laurel in gold, touched with brilliants. Her cloak is of black chiffon-velvet, with a cape collar of black fox. She slides this cloak from her shoulders onto the partition-seat at the right, and starts across towards the door at the left.*]

MRS. RITTER. [*Opening the door*] Are you up, Jenny?—Jenny! [*She closes the door again and crosses above the table at the left and over to the one below the piano. Here she sets down a few of the roses, then decides there is not sufficient room for all of them, and starts across to the table at the left. Ritter appears at the head of the stairs and starts down slowly. She sees him, and stops dead.*] Fred! [*She moves up towards the left of the center-door.*] You don't mean to tell me you've been home here,—and there I've been waiting at the hall since before ten o'clock. [*He wanders in through the center-door and leans against the piano, holding a lighted cigar in his hand.*] Why didn't you come back for me? Irene Colter had to bring me home. [*She starts to cry.*] Clara Sheppard *told* me she saw you there, so, naturally, I waited for you. And when you didn't come back, why, of course, right away—I thought something had happened to you. [*She cries into her handkerchief.*]

RITTER. [*Without moving, and in a toneless voice*] Something *has* happened to me. [*She looks at him apprehensively.*]

MRS. RITTER. What happened to you, Fred?

RITTER. [*Stonily, and moving down and across below the piano*] I've seen you act.

MRS. RITTER. What? [*He raises his left hand solemnly and continues to the corner of the piano nearest the window, where he leans. She moves down a bit after him.*] What's the matter, Fred,—did you have another of those spells that you had last night?

RITTER. Yes; only a great deal worse.

MRS. RITTER. Oh, isn't that dreadful! What do you think it is, dear?

RITTER. [*Turning slightly, and glancing at the violet easel and over at the anchor*] I don't know what it is. It looks like a *wake* to me. Who's dead?

MRS. RITTER. Dead?

RITTER. What are all these flowers doing here?

MRS. RITTER. Why, I imagine some of the ladies have been here from the show—to fix up a little surprise for *me*.

RITTER. They should have lighted a few candles, and completed the effect.

MRS. RITTER. But, these are just presents, Fred, from friends of ours.

RITTER. [*Straightening up, and moving across below the table*] They are tokens of sympathy, that's what they are. [*He crosses up and over above the table at the left.*]

MRS. RITTER. [*Following him over*] But, there's nobody *dead*, dear!

RITTER. [*Raising his left hand solemnly again*] Oh, yes there is! Oh yes!

MRS. RITTER. *Really*, dear! [*He turns, just back of the arm-chair, and pins her with a look.*]

RITTER. You're dead. [*She stands perfectly still, looking at him, wide-eyed.*] You died tonight,—down there on that stage at Horticultural Hall. And so did everybody that was up there with you.

MRS. RITTER. [*With a troubled, uncomprehending expression*] Why, how could I be dead, dear,—when I'm here,—talking to you? [*He stands looking straight ahead, smoking. She bursts out crying, and turns to the partition-seat at the right of the center-door.*] Oh, Fred! it's terrible to see you this way!

RITTER. [*Sweeping his hand across his brow and starting across below the table towards the right*] The human brain can only stand so much.

MRS. RITTER. [*Setting her roses down on the partition-seat*] You've just been working yourself to death! But nobody could tell you anything! [*She starts out into the left hallway for the telephone.*]

RITTER. [*Stopping over near the window and turning*] What are you going to do?

MRS. RITTER. [*Turning to him*] Why, I'm going to call Doctor Wentworth of course.

RITTER. What for?

MRS. RITTER. Why, because you *need* him!

RITTER. [*Taking a step or two towards her, between the piano and the table below it*] I won't see any doctor, now!

MRS. RITTER. [*Coming back through the center-door*] Now,—listen, Fred—

RITTER. [*Raising his hand, and crossing to the left*] I won't see any doctor, I tell you—there's nothing he can do for me: [*He stops above the arm-chair at the left and rests his hand upon the back of it.*] it's all been done. There's nothing left for me but to get out of town.

MRS. RITTER. [*Following him over*] Well, just let him come over and *see* you, dear.

RITTER. What would I let him come over and *see* me for? There's nothing the matter with me.

MRS. RITTER. Why, you're as pale as a ghost!

RITTER. That's nothing—I've had a scare.

MRS. RITTER. [*Solicitously*] What scared you, dear? [*He turns and looks at her.*]

RITTER. I was afraid every minute somebody was going to shoot *you*.

MRS. RITTER. [*After a bewildered pause*] But, why should anybody shoot *me*, darling?

RITTER. For trying to act. [*He moves forward and across in front of the table, to the right,—she watching him blankly.*] Making a laughing-stock of yourselves in front of the community.

MRS. RITTER. Didn't you like me, Fred?

RITTER. [*Casually, as he nears the window*] I did till I saw you act. [*He turns around to his right and leans on the piano. She moves over towards the table below the piano.*]

MRS. RITTER. [*Rather helplessly, as the situation dawns upon her*] Why, Mrs. Pampinelli said I was a great artist.

RITTER. [*With vast amusement*] Ha! [*Then he looks at his wife and speaks very exactly.*] Mrs. Pampinelli is perhaps the world's greatest NUT. [*Mrs. Pampinelli, standing back in the widow-alcove at the right, in a state of puzzled irresolution, reacts, physically, to this last observation, causing an abrupt movement of the drapery. But, neither Ritter nor his wife are looking in that direction at the moment.*]

MRS. RITTER. [*Laying the remaining roses on the table*] She says I ought to go on with the work.

RITTER. [*Dryly*] She meant the housework. [*He replaces his cigar in his mouth.*]

MRS. RITTER. [*Looking at him with a touch of resentment*] No, she didn't mean anything of the kind. She says I ought to go to New York. [*He takes the cigar from his mouth and looks at her keenly.*]

RITTER. And what would you do when you'd *get* there?

MRS. RITTER. Why, I'd go on the stage, of course.

RITTER. [*Very level*] How?

MRS. RITTER. Why, I'd go to the people that have charge of it.

RITTER. And, do you think they'd put you on the stage simply because you wanted to *go* on it?

MRS. RITTER. Well, Mrs. Pampinelli could give me a letter—

RITTER. Hum!

MRS. RITTER. So that I'd have it when I'd *get* there.

RITTER. That'd do you a lot of good. You'd find a *thousand* there ahead of you, with letters from Mrs. Pampinellis. Nobody in New York knows Mrs. Pampinelli; and if they did, it'd probably *kill* any chance that a person *might* have otherwise. [*Mrs. Pampinelli can contain herself no longer. She flips the window-drapery aside with a deft movement and stands looking at Ritter, from a great height. Mrs. Ritter, who is facing the window, utters an abrupt shriek of astonishment. Then Ritter turns, rather casually, to see the cause of his wife's agitation, and finds himself looking into the frozen eyes of Mrs. Pampinelli. He regards her rather impersonally, and then quietly reaches up and secures his collar and tie. She steps majestically from the window-alcove and moves a bit nearer to him, still holding him with an icy stare.*]

MRS. PAMPINELLI. [*After a devastating pause*] You creature.

RITTER. [*Turning smoothly away, to his left, as though he had been suddenly struck by something, in the right eye*] Another *actress*. [*He moves along a few steps to the left, in front of the table, then turns and speaks to Mrs. Pampinelli over his left shoulder.*] What did you do, come through the window?

MRS. PAMPINELLI. I've been *hiding* here.

RITTER. [*Resuming his walk over to the left*] I don't blame you,—after that show; I've been doing the same thing myself. [*He sits in the arm-chair over at the left.*]

MRS. RITTER. [*Who has been standing in a panic in the middle of the room, staring wide-eyed at Mrs. Pampinelli*] Oh, Mrs. Pampinelli,—you *didn't* hear what he's been saying?

MRS. PAMPINELLI. Every word. [*She very regally deposits her fan upon the piano, and Mrs. Ritter, turning to Ritter, makes a long, moaning sound.*]

MRS. RITTER. Now, Fred Ritter, you see what you've done! [*She bursts into tears, and comes down to the chair at the left of the table below the piano and sits down.*]

MRS. PAMPINELLI. [*Moving to a point above the table*] And I wouldn't have missed it. I'll know how to regard this gentleman in the future. I came home hurriedly with these few flowers as a little acknowledgment of the appreciation your work deserved; and all I hear is abuse; and a very crude, but very venomous attempt at satire. [*Mrs. Ritter weeps aloud.*] Control yourself, darling, I wouldn't please him.

RITTER. [*Quietly*] She's acting again.

MRS. PAMPINELLI. [*Withering him with a glance*] You barbarian! [*To Mrs. Ritter*] Pull yourself together, dear.

MRS. RITTER. Oh, I just *can't*, Mrs. Pampinelli.

MRS. PAMPINELLI. [*Addressing Ritter directly, and indicating Mrs. Ritter*] Look at the state of emotion you've got this poor girl into!

RITTER. She's an emotional actress. [*Mrs. Ritter bursts forth again.*]

MRS. PAMPINELLI. Savage! [*To Mrs. Ritter*] Let me get you something, darling.

MRS. RITTER. Call Jenny.

MRS. PAMPINELLI. Yes, dear. [*She crosses to a point just to the left of the middle of the room, then stops and calls toward the door at the left.*] Jenny dear, *SURPRISE!* [*Ritter listens, with a puzzled expression.*] Come here, Jenny,—SURPRISE! [*Ritter turns around in the chair, to his right, and looks at her curiously. She meets his eyes with steady bitterness. Then he shifts his gaze to his wife.*]

RITTER. Why didn't you take your make-up off?

MRS. RITTER. I forgot it,—I was so worried about you.

RITTER. You look like a Dutch squaw. [*She bursts into tears again.*]

MRS. PAMPINELLI. [*Hastening over to her*] Let her alone! Don't mind him, Paula.

RITTER. She's all made up! and it's coming off.

MRS. PAMPINELLI. Well, what if it is?

RITTER. [*Settling back into the arm-chair*] I don't want to be reminded of that show. [*Jenny enters hurriedly from the door at the left.*]

MRS. PAMPINELLI. Mrs. Ritter is ill, Jenny. [*Jenny comes quickly across, above the table at the left.*]

MRS. RITTER. [*Half turning to her*] My smelling-salts, Jenny.

MRS. PAMPINELLI. [*Standing back of Mrs. Ritter*] Her smelling-salts, dear.

JENNY. [*Hurrying out through the center-door*] Yes, mam.

MRS. RITTER. They're in my bureau-basket.

MRS. PAMPINELLI. [*Turning and calling after Jenny*] In her bureau-basket, Jenny.

JENNY. [*Running up the stairs*] Yes, mam, I know where they are.

MRS. PAMPINELLI. [*Gathering up the roses from the table*] Let me take these flowers out of your way, dear. You've been treated abominably. Although your husband's attitude is entirely consistent with that of the average husband's, after his wife has distinguished herself. [*Ritter makes a little sound of amusement, and she glares at him.*] And any observations of Mr. Ritter's to the contrary, you *did* distinguish yourself tonight, Paula. [*She turns to her right and puts the roses on the piano.*]

RITTER. [*Sitting away down in the arm-chair, smoking*] So did the Cherry Sisters. [*Mrs. Ritter weeps again.*]

MRS. PAMPINELLI. [*Turning back again from the piano to Mrs. Ritter*] We are not talking to you at all, sir. [*Mrs. Ritter has a slight coughing spell.*]

MRS. RITTER. Will you get me a drink of water, please?

MRS. PAMPINELLI. Certainly, darling, where is it?

MRS. RITTER. You'll find it just inside the breakfast-room. [*Mrs. Pampinelli sails across the room towards the left door. Just as she is passing back of Ritter's chair, he turns and looks at her, and the excessive grandeur of her manner causes him to burst out laughing. But she simply freezes him with a look and goes out through the left door. He continues to laugh; and Mrs. Ritter, not having seen the cause of his laughter, stops crying and turns and looks at him, very troubled.*] Fred Ritter, you're acting to me tonight—just like a man that'd be losing his mind! [*He looks over at her.*] I really thought that was what was the matter with you when I first came in!

RITTER. [*Very confidentially*] Listen—When I didn't lose my mind watching that show tonight, I couldn't go nutty if I tried.

MRS. RITTER. Well, if anybody else comes here tonight, you just keep that kind of talk to yourself. There were lots of people there that thought it was wonderful. Look at all these flowers.

RITTER. These flowers were all paid for long before anybody saw that show. [*There is a staccato tap at the front door-bell. Jenny is hurrying down the stairs with the smelling-salts.*]

MRS. RITTER. [*Rising, and trying to fix herself up a bit*] Well, that's only your opinion. [*She starts for the center-door.*] This is very likely Nelly Fell. [*Turning back to him as she nears the center-door*] Now, don't you say anything to *her*, remember! She likes you.

MRS. FELL. [*In the right hallway*] No, I think I can manage, Theodore. [*Jenny hands Mrs. Ritter the smelling-salts, at the center-door.*]

MRS. RITTER. Thanks, Jenny.

JENNY. You're welcome. [*She hurries out into the right hallway, and Mrs. Ritter comes forward to the chair below the piano, sniffing the salts. Ritter rises and saunters around and up to the left of the arm-chair.*]

MRS. FELL. You can close that door, if you will! Couldn't wait for you, Jenny! [*She rushes in from the right hallway.*] I'm too much excited! [*She plants herself in the center-door, holding aloft in her right hand a beautiful basket of tulips, and in her left, a huge bouquet of violets.*] Well, here *I* am, with *my* frankincense and myrrh! [*She gives an hysterical giggle and teeters forward towards Mrs. Ritter.*] Oh, there you are, Frederick Ritter! We thought something had happened to you! Pauline, dear child, I've come to worship at your shrine. [*She places the basket of tulips down on the floor to the left of Mrs. Ritter, then straightens up, regards Mrs. Ritter, giggles frantically, and looks over at Ritter.*]

MRS. RITTER. [*Laughing wanly, and trying generally not to appear as though she'd been crying*] You've been very sweet.

MRS. FELL. Not half so sweet as you were on that stage tonight! [*Speaking confidentially, and with great conviction*] Dear child, you're made! Absolutely made! [*Turning to Ritter*] Isn't she, Frederick? [*But he's busy getting rid of some ashes in the fireplace, so she returns to Mrs. Ritter.*] It's one of those overnight things that one reads about! [*She picks up the basket of tulips from the floor and teeters around above the table.*] Dear me, look at this wilderness of flowers! [*She sets the basket on the table.*]

MRS. RITTER. [*Trying not to cry*] Yes, yes, aren't they beautiful! [*She darts a look at Ritter.*]

MRS. FELL. [*Rapturously*] Not another word until I've kissed you! [*She kisses her on the left side of the head.*] Oh, you sweet child! [*She shakes Mrs. Ritter by the shoulders.*] what can I *say* to you! [*Then she teeters to the middle of the room, addressing Ritter directly.*] See here, young man! Why aren't you just *pelting* your wife with these flowers? [*He tries to hide his appreciation of the situation by turning away his head.*] Answer me! [*He bursts out laughing, and Nelly teeters back towards Mrs. Ritter.*] My dear, the man is so pleased he can't talk! [*Ritter laughs a little more.*] And if you were any other woman but his wife, Paula, he'd be sending you mash-notes! [*Ritter begins to laugh again, and Nelly teeters towards him.*] Oh, you can laugh all you like, Frederick Ritter, but you can't fool Nelly Fell! [*She comes back towards Mrs. Ritter, addressing her.*] I've had three husbands,—I know their tricks. [*She places her finger on Mrs. Ritter's shoulder.*] Pauline, dear child, you may be sure that that young man is proud of you tonight if he never was before. [*Mrs. Ritter tries to laugh.*] And when he gets you alone—[*Mrs. Ritter's attempt at laughter is instantly abandoned, and she gives a startled glance toward Ritter, who turns away to his left and goes up towards the mantelpiece.*] Oh, when he gets you alone! [*Mrs. Fell turns slowly and looks toward Ritter, with a roguish expression and a measured shaking of her finger at him.*] He's going to tell you you were the loveliest thing that ever stepped on a stage. If he hasn't done so already. Have you, Frederick? [*She looks at him with a mischievous eye.*] Have you? [*He laughs, at the irony of the situation. She crosses towards him.*] Come on, 'fess up!—I know the position is difficult! [*He laughs hard, and she laughs with him; then turns back to Mrs. Ritter. Jenny comes in from the right hallway.*] You see, my dear, the man is so pleased he can't talk! [*She sees Jenny passing along the hallway and steps quickly up to the center-door.*] Oh, Jenny dear! Will you take these violets out and put them in some water.

JENNY. [*Taking the violets*] Yes, mam. [*Mrs. Pampinelli enters at the left door, with a glass of water.*]

MRS. FELL. I'm afraid they'll be all withered. [*Jenny continues on into the left hallway. Mrs. Fell turns around into the room again.*] Where's Mrs. P.? [*Sees Mrs. Pampinelli*] Oh, there you are! I was just wondering where you were.

MRS. PAMPINELLI. [*Crossing above the table at the left, towards Mrs. Ritter*] Did you get the smelling-salts, Jenny?

JENNY. Yes, mam, I gave them to Mrs. Ritter. [*She goes out at the left hallway.*]

MRS. RITTER. Yes, Betty, I have them.

MRS. FELL. [*Coming a step or two forward*] Well, Betty, you see we managed to get them all here.

MRS. PAMPINELLI. [*Back of the table below the piano, and at Mrs. Ritter's left*] Here, try and drink this, Paula. [*Mrs. Ritter takes the water and tries to drink it; and Mrs. Pampinelli leans solicitously over her. There is a pause.*]

MRS. FELL. [*Coming anxiously down at Mrs. Ritter's left*] What's the matter?— [*She looks at Mrs. Pampinelli.*] Is Paula sick?

MRS. PAMPINELLI. [*Straightening up, and very imperiously*] The *critic*—has been giving his impressions of our play.

MRS. FELL. Who? [*She turns towards Ritter.*] This critic here, you mean? [*She indicates Ritter and then looks at Mrs. Pampinelli. Mrs. Pampinelli inclines her head, with the suggestion of a derisive smile, and passes up to the center-door. Mrs. Fell crosses quickly towards Ritter.*] What have you been saying, Frederick Ritter?—Huh?

MRS. RITTER. [*Laying the glass of water down on the table*] Oh, what does it matter, Nelly, what he's been saying!

MRS. FELL. [*Turning sharply to Mrs. Ritter*] What?

MRS. RITTER. [*Trying not to cry*] I say—I say [*She bursts into tears.*] I say what does it matter what he's been saying!

MRS. FELL. It doesn't matter in the least, as far as I'm concerned—[*Mrs. Pampinelli turns at the center-door and comes forward slowly in the middle of the room.*] there's only one thing he *could* say, if he told the truth.

MRS. PAMPINELLI. [*Laying her hand on Mrs. Fell's left arm*] Eleanor, dear child,—husbands are not always particular about telling the truth—where the abilities of their wives are concerned. If *I* had listened to the promptings of my own soul, instead of to my husband, when I was a younger woman, I should in all probability be one of the leading figures in the American Theatre today. But I was fool enough, like a lot of other women, to believe that my husband had my welfare at heart,—when the fact of the matter was, as I see it now, when it's too late,—he was simply jealous of my artistic promise. [*The cuckoo-clock strikes the midnight hour. Ritter turns and looks up at it, then glances at Mrs. Pampinelli. She is looking up at the clock distrustfully. Mrs. Fell raises her eyes discreetly to it, then drops them to the floor.*] Why, the night I played Hazel Kirke, I had my best friends in tears: yet, when I returned from the hall, and the entire town of Cohoes ringing with my name,—my husband had the effrontery to tell me that I was so terrific he was obliged to leave the hall before the end of the first act. So,—[*She turns to Mrs. Ritter.*] if this gentleman here has set himself up as your critic, Paula,—remember *my* story,—the actress without honor in her own house. [*She sweeps across below the piano to the window.*] Is my car out here, Nelly?

MRS. FELL. [*Moving over a bit towards Mrs. Ritter*] Yes, it's there. I told Matthew he needn't bother coming back for me, that you'd take me home. [*Mrs. Ritter begins to cry softly, and Mrs. Fell steps to her left and puts her hand on her shoulder.*] Don't do that, Paula. [*She turns sharply and goes towards Ritter.*] What was the matter with that performance, Frederick Ritter?

RITTER. [*Over at the left, below the mantelpiece*] Why, they didn't even know their lines!

MRS. RITTER. [*Straightening up abruptly and looking at him, reproachfully*] Oh!

MRS. PAMPINELLI. [*Turning sharply from the window*] That is a falsehood! They ran over every line last night, right here in this room,—and they knew—practically all of them.

RITTER. What good was that, if they couldn't remember them on the stage.

MRS. RITTER and MRS. PAMPINELLI, together.

> MRS. RITTER. [*To Ritter*] I *could* remember them on the stage! [*Turning to Mrs. Pampinelli*] I never missed *one* line!

> MRS. PAMPINELLI. [*To Ritter*] They *could* remember them on the stage!

MRS. PAMPINELLI. [*To Mrs. Ritter*] Not a line.

RITTER. She and that other woman sat there blinking at the audience like a couple of sparrow-hawks.

MRS. PAMPINELLI. They did nothing of the kind.

MRS. FELL. Of course they didn't!

RITTER. [*Speaking directly to Mrs. Fell*] How do you know? *You* weren't out there.

MRS. FELL. I could see them through the scenery, couldn't I? And they didn't look anything *like* a couple of sparrow-hawks,—as you say.

MRS. PAMPINELLI. [*Contemptuously*] Well, as I have never seen a couple of sparrow-hawks, I cannot appreciate the comparison.

RITTER. Well, you'd have seen a couple tonight, if you'd been with me.

MRS. RITTER. Oh, don't argue with him, Betty! He's only trying to be smart.

RITTER. Why didn't one of them *say* something?

MRS. PAMPINELLI. What could they have said?

RITTER. Why, any commonplace! It'd have been better than just sitting there blinking. [*Mrs. Ritter weeps.*]

MRS. PAMPINELLI. One can't be commonplace in high comedy.

RITTER. Was that what it was?

MRS. PAMPINELLI. [*Bitterly*] What did you *think* it was?

RITTER. [*Turning and going up to the center-door*] *You* tell her, Nelly; I haven't got the heart.

MRS. FELL. [*Moving a little towards the right*] You bold thing. [*Nelly is wearing the gown she wore in the preceding act, and a heavy cloak of old-rose-colored velvet. She lays her hand on Mrs. Ritter's left shoulder.*] Don't let him upset you this way, Paula. [*There is a little pause. Ritter turns at the center-door and comes forward again at the left.*]

MRS. PAMPINELLI. [*Picking up her fan from the piano*] I suppose *you* would have eclipsed Edwin Booth, if *you* had been up there.

RITTER. Well, I'd have known better than to sit there blinking at the audience.

MRS. RITTER. [*Turning sharply to him*] I didn't *blink* at the audience.

MRS. FELL. Don't answer him, honey.

MRS. PAMPINELLI. What could they have done under the circumstances?

RITTER. Why, they could have covered it up!—if they'd had any brains.

MRS. PAMPINELLI. Covered it up with *what?*

RITTER. Why, with anything! Impromptu conversation! [*Mrs. Fell looks at Mrs. Pampinelli and smiles pityingly.*]

MRS. PAMPINELLI. And have the audience *laugh* at them?

RITTER. They laughed anyhow, didn't they?

MRS. FELL. [*Taking a step or two towards him*] That was not their fault!

RITTER. [*To Nelly*] Whose fault *was it?*

MRS. PAMPINELLI. [*Imperiously, and moving over to a point above the table at which Mrs. Ritter is sitting*] It was Mr. Spindler's fault.

RITTER. Mr. Spindler.

MRS. PAMPINELLI. He promised to attend to the various properties and he did *not* attend to them.—There was supposed to be a pen and ink on the desk for Mrs. Rush to leave a note for Doctor Arlington;—and when Paula sat down to write the note, there was no pen—and no ink. So she simply had to go on sitting there until Mr. Spearing went off and got them.

RITTER. I thought he'd left town.

MRS. FELL. Oh, he wasn't gone so very long, Frederick Ritter!

MRS. PAMPINELLI. [*Bitterly, to Mrs. Fell*] Not five minutes.

RITTER. I thought the show'ud be over before he'd get back.

MRS. PAMPINELLI. The door wouldn't open when he attempted to go back, so he was obliged to go around to the other side. [*She illustrates the circumstance by waving her fan in a circular gesture about the table. Ritter bursts out laughing. Nelly glares at him, then looks to Mrs. Pampinelli, who, with a deadly, level look, turns and moves haughtily up towards the center-door.*]

RITTER. What happened to the skinny guy's mustache, that it kept falling off every other line?

MRS. PAMPINELLI. [*Turning to him, up near the center-door*] It only fell off twice, don't exaggerate. [*Ritter laughs again.*]

MRS. FELL. You bold thing!

RITTER. How many times was it *supposed* to fall off?

MRS. PAMPINELLI. Well, what if it fell off a dozen times,—everybody knew it wasn't real! [*He roars.*]

MRS. FELL. It's a lucky thing for you, Frederick Ritter, that you're not *my* husband!

RITTER. [*Quietly*] That goes both ways, Nelly.

MRS. FELL. [*Moving across towards him*] Well,—when you do something that you'll get so many flowers that my limousine will have to make three trips to get them to the various hospitals,—we may pay more attention to what you have to say. [*She turns away and moves back towards the center of the room, where Mrs. Pampinelli is just moving forward from the center-door.*]

RITTER. I suppose most of the audience have gone with the flowers, haven't they? [*Nelly whirls round to retort, but Mrs. Pampinelli lays a restraining hand upon her right arm.*]

MRS. PAMPINELLI. [*With immortal authority*] Don't answer him, Eleanor— "Envy loves a lofty mark." The next time we have a part that calls for a very limited intelligence, we'll engage Mr. Ritter for it. [*She moves a little down to the right towards Mrs. Ritter.*]

MRS. FELL. [*Looking at Ritter*] Now!

RITTER. [*Casually*] Well, if you do, he'll know how to walk across the stage without tripping every other step.

MRS. FELL. Who tripped every other step?

RITTER. [*Indicating his wife*] The weeping-willow there. [*Mrs. Ritter begins to weep afresh.*]

MRS. FELL. It's a wonder to me you're not afraid to lie so!

RITTER. She tripped when she first came through the door! I was looking right at her.

MRS. PAMPINELLI. [*Turning to him*] She didn't *fall*, did she?

RITTER. No, but it looked for a while there as though she were going to. [*Mrs. Ritter's weeping becomes audible again.*] I very nearly had heart failure.

MRS. PAMPINELLI. [*Laying her hand on Paula's shoulder*] Don't mind him, Paula.

RITTER. She tripped when she came *on* the stage, she tripped when she went *off*, and she tripped over the rug when she went over to the desk!

MRS. PAMPINELLI. [*With measured finality*] She didn't trip any oftener than anybody else. [*He laughs.*]

MRS. FELL. [*Directly to Ritter*] No, nor half so often as some of the others,— [*Turning towards Mrs. Pampinelli*] now that you speak of it! [*She turns and goes up to the hallway.*]

MRS. PAMPINELLI. I will admit that Mr. Hossefrosse is a bit unsteady,—but that is due to his weak ankles.

RITTER. What was the star's unsteadiness due to?

MRS. RITTER. The rugs!

RITTER. [Looking at her keenly] What?

MRS. RITTER and MRS. PAMPINELLI, together.

> MRS. RITTER. The rugs.

> MRS. PAMPINELLI. [Moving to the center of the room] The rugs!

MRS. PAMPINELLI. Those funny rugs—that they have down there. We didn't use them at the rehearsals,—and, naturally, when it came to the performance,—Paula wasn't accustomed to them.

RITTER. She was accustomed to rugs at home, wasn't she?

MRS. PAMPINELLI. [Tersely] Well, she wasn't at home on the stage.

RITTER. [With a gesture of complete acquiesence, and moving up towards the center-door] That's my argument in a nutshell. [Mrs. Pampinelli stands frozen in the middle of the room, with an expression very much as though she were trying mentally to assassinate him. He comes back down again at the left, to his former position.] Why, I couldn't hear two-thirds of what she said.

MRS. PAMPINELLI. Well, evidently there were many people there who could hear what she said, for they laughed at all her points. [She turns and goes to the piano, where she picks up several roses. Mrs. Fell comes forward through the center-door and down towards the piano.]

RITTER. I wanted to laugh, too, but I was afraid somebody'd turn around and see me.

MRS. PAMPINELLI. [Turning to Mrs. Ritter] Are you ready, Nelly?

MRS. FELL. Yes, I'm ready.

MRS. RITTER. Are you going, Betty?

MRS. PAMPINELLI. Yes, I must, darling, it's getting late. [She places her hand on Mrs. Ritter's shoulder.] Good night, dear. [She passes up towards the center-door.]

MRS. RITTER. Good night, Betty.

MRS. FELL. [Laying her hand on Mrs. Ritter's shoulder] Good night, Paula child.

MRS. RITTER. Good night, Nelly. [Nelly follows Mrs. Pampinelli.]

MRS. PAMPINELLI. [*Stopping in the center-door and turning to Ritter*] Perhaps, at our *next* performance,—Mr. Ritter will favor us with the benefit of some of his suggestions. [*She regards him with a touch of lofty amusement. He turns his head towards her and looks at her with a kind of mischievous squint.*]

RITTER. [*Quite pleasantly*] There aren't going to be any more performances, Mrs. Pampinelli, as far as anybody in *this* house is concerned.

MRS. PAMPINELLI. [*After a steady pause*] No? [*He inclines his head in quiet emphasis.*]

RITTER. Not until there's a change in the management. [*There is another taut pause.*]

MRS. PAMPINELLI. [*Coldly*] Really? [*He inclines his head again.*] Then, I'm afraid we sha'n't have you with us, Mr. Ritter.

RITTER. [*Smiling*] I know very well you won't have *me* with you. And as far as Mrs. Ritter's concerned,—she's got a very good home here—and I love her; and any time she feels any dramatic instinct coming on, there's a very nice roomy attic upstairs, and she can go up there and lock the door, and nobody'll ever see or hear her. But if she ever gets mixed up again in anything like that atrocity I saw tonight,—I'm through. [*He speaks the last words with quiet definiteness, and turns towards the door at the left.*] And she'll get killed in the bargain. [*He hits the door open with the palm of his hand and goes out. There is a slight pause: then Nelly Fell crosses quickly towards the mantelpiece, addressing Ritter as she goes.*]

MRS. FELL. Why, Fred Ritter!—I've heard you say yourself that you were in *favor* of a Little Theatre in this city!

RITTER. [*Coming in again through the door at the left, carrying his overcoat, derby and scarf*] So I am! I say so again. [*He stops inside the door.*] But in the light of that cataclysm tonight, you'll pardon me if I add, that I do not see the connection.

MRS. PAMPINELLI. [*Stepping forward to the middle of the room and challenging him with a lift of her head and brows*] What did you *expect* to *see*, Mr. Ritter,—a finished performance from a group of comparative amateurs?

RITTER. I expected to see something almost as bad as what I saw;—that's the reason I *fainted* last night and was unconscious for twenty-four hours at the prospect of it. [*He turns to Mrs. Fell and speaks quite colloquially.*] And that's the first time in my life I've ever fainted. [*Nelly just gives him a look and turns her head away.*]

MRS. RITTER. Don't mind him, Betty,—he's only trying to show off.

MRS. PAMPINELLI. [*With bitter amusement*] No, but I'm a bit *curious*—to know just *how* Mr. Ritter would expect to *accomplish* the establishment of a Little

Theatre here, unless through the medium of such performances as this one this evening. How else is our local talent to be discovered—or developed?

RITTER. Well, I'm equally curious, Mrs. Pampinelli, as to your exact *qualifications*—as a discoverer or developer of talent for the theatre.

MRS. PAMPINELLI. That is a very familiar attitude. People who *do* things— are constantly having their ability to do them called into question. [*She moves a step further forward and towards Mrs. Ritter.*]

RITTER. I'm afraid that's something you've read somewhere. [*She glares at him.*]

MRS. PAMPINELLI. The theatre is a matter of instinct.

RITTER. The theatre is a matter of qualifications,—the same as any other profession; and it will only be *through* those particular qualifications that your Little Theatre will ever be brought about. [*He crosses over in front of Mrs. Fell and up towards the center-door.*]

MRS. PAMPINELLI. Well, perhaps you will come to the rescue;—you seem so familiar with the various necessities of the Little Theatre. [*He stops, just to the left of the center-door, and looks at Mrs. Pampinelli straight.*]

RITTER. [*Quietly*] I am also familiar, Mrs. Pampinelli, with a little remark that Mr. Napoleon made on one occasion, a long time ago;—about the immorality of assuming a position for which one is unqualified. [*There is a pause,—he settles his coat on his arm, then moves slowly out through the center-door into the hallway: while Mrs. Pampinelli, with an expression of eternal exclusion, moves over between the piano and the table towards the window.*]

MRS. RITTER. [*Turning*] Fred Ritter, where are you going?

RITTER. [*Lighting his cigar in the hallway, just outside the center-door*] I haven't the faintest idea. But I shouldn't be surprised if I'd go on the stage.

MRS. FELL. [*Standing back of the arm-chair at the left*] One star is enough in the family.

RITTER. [*Bowing very graciously to her*] Applause—[*She turns away and looks straight ahead. Then Ritter bows towards Mrs. Pampinelli.*] and great laughter—[*Mrs. Pampinelli isn't looking at him, but she knows that that is meant for her, so she simply moves another step or two towards the window. Mrs. Ritter turns to see what Ritter is doing. He takes a step and leans forward towards her, speaking rather confidentially.*] followed by booing. [*She turns back again and starts to cry, while he continues out into the right hallway and up the stairs. As he mounts the stairs, he holds aloft his lighted cigar, after the fashion of a zealous bearer of the torch.*]

MRS. PAMPINELLI. [*Picking up the orchids from the table below the window*] Paula, you should have Jenny put these orchids in water; they keep ever so long in a cool place. [*She comes across towards the left, below the piano.*]

MRS. RITTER. Will you call her, Nelly?

MRS. FELL. [*Crossing to meet Mrs. Pampinelli*] Give them to me, Betty, I'll take them out to her. [*Mrs. Pampinelli gives her the orchids.*]

MRS. PAMPINELLI. Tell her to put them in a cool place. [*Nelly starts up for the center-door. The telephone-bell rings.*]

MRS. RITTER. Will you answer that, Nelly?

MRS. FELL. [*Setting the orchids down on the chair in the left hallway*] Certainly, darling.

MRS. PAMPINELLI. [*Standing back of Mrs. Ritter's chair*] If it's anything concerning the play, I shall be at home on Tuesday at two.

MRS. FELL. [*At the telephone*] Yes?—Yes?—Who?—Oh,—well, wait just one moment, please.

MRS. PAMPINELLI. What is it?

MRS. FELL. [*Holding the transmitter against her bosom and leaning over the partition towards Mrs. Pampinelli*] It's the Star Moving Picture Company.

MRS. PAMPINELLI. What do they want?

MRS. FELL. They want the address of Mrs. Ritter's manager. [*Mrs. Pampinelli gives a quick look at Mrs. Ritter.*]

MRS. PAMPINELLI. [*To Mrs. Ritter*] I anticipated this. [*She goes quickly towards the center-door, laying her fan and roses on the left partition-seat, as she passes out into the hallway.*] Give it to me, Nelly. [*Nelly hands her the telephone, and, picking up the orchids from the chair, tiptoes back of Mrs. Pampinelli and in through the center-door.*]

MRS. FELL. [*In an excited whisper to Mrs. Ritter*] What did I tell you! [*She giggles nervously, shakes her finger at Mrs. Ritter, and then watches Mrs. Pampinelli eagerly.*]

MRS. PAMPINELLI. [*Into the telephone*] Hello-hello—This is Mrs. Ritter's manager speaking. Mrs. Pampinelli. Pampinelli. Mrs. J. *Duro* Pampinelli. Capital P—a—m, p—i—n, e—double l—i.—Correct. Yes—I see—I see.— Well, how do you mean, a thousand dollars, a thousand dollars a day, or a thous—I see. Well, just one moment, please. [*She lowers the telephone and leans towards Mrs. Ritter, speaking in a subdued tone.*] The Star Moving Picture Company wants to know if Mrs. Ritter will appear in a special production of tonight's play before the camera.

MRS. FELL. [*Narrowing her left eye*] What's the figure?

MRS. PAMPINELLI. One thousand dollars per week.

MRS. FELL. [*Definitely*] Fifteen hundred.

MRS. PAMPINELLI. [*Into the telephone*] Hello-hello!

MRS. RITTER. [*Rising*] Maybe I'd better talk to them.

MRS. FELL. [*Suggesting with a gesture that she be quiet and resume her chair*] Please, dear. [*Mrs. Ritter meekly sits down again.*]

MRS. PAMPINELLI. [*Into the telephone*] Why, I'm sorry,—but Mrs. Ritter does not appear under fifteen hundred dollars per week.

MRS. FELL. [*Watching her shrewdly*] Net! [*Mrs. Pampinelli turns and looks at her sharply, and Nelly emphasizes what she said by inclining her head: then Mrs. Pampinelli speaks into the telephone again.*]

MRS. PAMPINELLI. Net.

MRS. FELL. [*To Mrs. Pampinelli*] It's a bargain at that. [*She nods towards Mrs. Ritter.*]

MRS. PAMPINELLI. [*Into telephone*] Twelve-fifty?

MRS. FELL. No compromise.

MRS. PAMPINELLI. [*Into telephone*] Well, just one moment. [*Covering the transmitter and speaking to Mrs. Fell*] Twelve-fifty is offered.

MRS. FELL. [*Definitely*] Fifteen hundred dollars. They'll lift it.

MRS. PAMPINELLI. [*Turning back to the telephone*] Why, I'm very sorry,—but Mrs. Ritter positively does not appear under fifteen hundred dollars. [*Nelly inclines her head towards her.*] Net. Well, how do you mean satisfactory? Satisfactory at our figure? [*Mrs. Pampinelli glances at Mrs. Fell and Mrs. Fell glances at Mrs. Ritter.*]

MRS. FELL. [*To Mrs. Pampinelli*] Sign!

MRS. PAMPINELLI. [*Into the telephone*] Very well, then,—signed at fifteen hundred dollars per week,—

MRS. FELL. Net!

MRS. PAMPINELLI. [*Into the telephone*] Net! And Mrs. Ritter appears. [*She stands holding the telephone and listening.*]

MRS. FELL. [*Whirling round and teetering down to Paula*] Our STAR! I always said it! [*She shakes Mrs. Ritter by the shoulders.*] I always said it! [*She whirls round and teeters up towards the center-door.*] Haven't I always said it, Betty? [*Mrs. Pampinelli is listening on the telephone, and tries, by dint of thrusting the telephone towards Nelly, to silence her. But Nelly is irrepressible.*] That it was only a question of time? [*She turns and flies down towards Mrs. Ritter again.*] We must telephone Mrs. Livingston at once, Paula!

MRS. PAMPINELLI. Be quiet, Nelly, be quiet!

MRS. FELL. [*Rushing up towards the center-door again*] She'll be so interested! We must call up Mrs. Livingston right away, Betty!

MRS. PAMPINELLI. Please, Nelly! [*Nelly is silenced. Mrs. Pampinelli listens sharply, Nelly and Mrs. Ritter watching her; and there is a dead pause.*] Beg pardon? [*There is another slight pause; and then Mrs. Pampinelli utters an abrupt shriek and sets down the telephone.*]

MRS. FELL. What is it, Betty? [*Mrs. Pampinelli looks at her, then straight ahead.*]

MRS. PAMPINELLI. [*With venomous enunciation*] It's Ritter! [*Mrs. Ritter rises slowly.*]

MRS. FELL. Ritter? [*Mrs. Pampinelli doesn't stir.*]

MRS. RITTER. [*Addressing Mrs. Pampinelli*] Fred?

MRS. PAMPINELLI. I recognized his voice. [*She moves along the left hallway and comes in through the center-door and forward, a little to the left of the center of the room.*]

MRS. FELL. [*Up just to the right of the center-door*] Why, where is he?

MRS. RITTER. [*Beginning to cry*] He must be on the extension upstairs. [*Nelly listens keenly.*]

MRS. FELL. It is he; I hear him laughing. [*She crosses down to the door at the left.*]

MRS. PAMPINELLI. [*Taking a step towards Mrs. Ritter*] Sit down, Paula. [*Mrs. Ritter sits down, rests her elbows on the table and weeps bitterly. Nelly stops over at the door and turns.*]

MRS. FELL. [*Positively*] Paula,—if he were *my* husband, I should lose no time in having him arrested. [*She goes out, at the left door.*]

MRS. PAMPINELLI. [*Standing back of Mrs. Ritter's chair*] Paula dear, I do hope that you are not going to allow Mr. Ritter's flippancies to discourage you. [*Paula clasps her hands in her lap and looks tearfully at the backs of them.*] The way of the essential artist is always hard; and so very frequently the most serious obstacles are those to be encountered at home.

MRS. RITTER. But, I feel so unsuccessful.

MRS. PAMPINELLI. I know, dear—I know exactly how you feel. But you must *go on.* Just remember that art is the highest expression of truth,—and you cannot fail. For you have everything in your favor, Paula.

MRS. RITTER. [*Weakly*] Thank you.

MRS. PAMPINELLI. And the masses need you, dear; you are an altogether *new note* in the theatre.

MRS. RITTER. But—I don't know whether Fred'll *want* me to go on any more—[*Mrs. Pampinelli suddenly becomes very still and stoney, and looks down at Mrs. Ritter with merciless inquiry. Mrs. Ritter senses the change and turns hastily to explain.*] the way he spoke.

MRS. PAMPINELLI. And, do you mean that you will allow him to *stop* you, Paula?

MRS. RITTER. [*Breaking down under Mrs. Pampinelli's frozen amusement*] Well, of course, he's my *husband*, Betty. [*She cries. Mrs. Pampinelli regards her with a kind of pained toleration; and settles her cloak, preparatory to going.*]

MRS. PAMPINELLI. Very well, then, Paula—if you feel that way about it, I should advise you to keep him; and I shan't waste any more of my time encouraging you. [*She sweeps around to her left and up towards the center-door.*] There are far too many who are only too *willing* to make the necessary sacrifices without being urged. [*She picks up her fan and roses from the partition-seat, lays them across her left arm, and turns regnantly to Mrs. Ritter.*] Only remember this, Paula,—there will be actresses when husbands are a thing of the past. [*She sweeps out through the center-door and out into the right hallway. There is a slight pause; then Nelly Fell comes in at the left door. She misses Mrs. Pampinelli.*]

MRS. FELL. Where is Mrs. P., Paula?

MRS. RITTER. She's just gone out to the car, Nelly.

MRS. FELL. [*Stooping to pick up one of the chrysanthemums from the floor*] Do you mind if I take one of these flowers, Paula? [*She stands in the middle of the room, holding it, and looking at Mrs. Ritter.*] I want it for my dramatic shrine.

MRS. RITTER. You can take them all if you like.

MRS. FELL. Why, what would *you* do, dear?

MRS. RITTER. I don't want them.

MRS. FELL. [*Crossing towards her*] Now, you mustn't feel like that, Paula Ritter.

MRS. RITTER. [*Having all she can do to keep from crying*] I just can't help it.

MRS. FELL. I see in your husband's attitude—nothing but a desperate attempt to save his home;—for he *must* know what your performance tonight will inevitably lead to. [*Mrs. Ritter turns with a puzzled expression and looks at her.*]

MRS. RITTER. I don't understand what you mean, Nelly.

MRS. FELL. Why, you must go to New York, dear; you can do nothing dramatically here.

MRS. RITTER. But, I have a husband.

MRS. FELL. [*Very casually*] Every married woman has that cross, darling. But you mustn't let it stand in the way of your career; he would very soon eliminate *you*, if you stood in the way of *his*.

MRS. RITTER. But, I don't like the thought of breaking up his home, Nelly. [*Nelly gives a hard, knowing little laugh.*]

MRS. FELL. Don't be unnecessarily sacrificial, darling. I made that mistake with my first *two* husbands; but I was *wiser* with the third. And I said to him, immediately we returned from the church, I said, "Now, Leonard, you and I have just been made one; and *I* am that one." [*She touches herself on the breastbone with her forefinger, then touches Paula on the left shoulder.*] And it worked out beautifully. So be sensible, darling. [*She skips up towards the hallway.*] I must run along, Mrs. Pampinelli's waiting! [*She teeters out through the center-door into the right hallway.*] Cheerio, Paula darling!

MRS. RITTER. Good night.

MRS. FELL. Cheerio! [*She giggles and vanishes into the right hallway. Mrs. Ritter sits still for a second, looking from side to side, at nothing, particularly, and presently gets up. The horseshoe of "SUCCESS" over in front of the mantelpiece catches her eye, and she wanders slowly towards it. But the irony of it all overcomes her and she commences to cry again. Ritter appears at the head of the stairs and starts down. She turns and looks at him, as he comes through the center-door.*]

MRS. RITTER. Fred Ritter, those women will never come inside that door again, the way you talked to them. [*He moves to the piano and leans against it.*]

RITTER. Well, I don't suppose that'll make very much difference.

MRS. RITTER. [*Looking straight ahead*] Well, it *should* make a difference.

RITTER. They'd hardly come here to see *me*, anyway.

MRS. RITTER. Well, they'd come to see me.

RITTER. But *you* won't be here. [*She turns and looks at him blankly.*]

MRS. RITTER. Why,—what—what do you mean, I won't be here?

RITTER. [*With a touch of delicacy*] Why, aren't you going on with *The Work*?

MRS. RITTER. Well, I don't want to go unless you *want* me to.

RITTER. But, I *do* want you to. I don't think a talent like yours should be hidden; [*He looks straight out, thoughtfully.*] it's too unique.

MRS. RITTER. I thought you said a while ago you didn't like me?

RITTER. [*Raising his left hand and crossing over and down in front of her towards the arm-chair at the left*] You mustn't hold me responsible for what I said a while ago—[*He stops back of the arm-chair and rests his hand upon the back of it.*] I was panic-stricken at the thought of having my home broken up. [*She moves down to the center of the room.*] But I've been thinking it over upstairs, and I've concluded that it's more important that the world should see you act, than that I should have a home to come to.

MRS. RITTER. But, I don't like the thought of breaking up your home, Fred.

RITTER. [*Raising his right hand to her with a touch of solemnity*] You mustn't consider me in the matter at all, dear. Every great gift has its victim—and I am, in a way, rather happy—to find myself chosen the victim of yours.

MRS. RITTER. What would *you* do, if I were to go?

RITTER. [*With the faintest shade of classic pose*] I'd go with you; you'd need someone to look after the flowers—see that they got to the various hospitals all right.

MRS. RITTER. [*Looking away out*] I might not like it, after I'd get there.

RITTER. Maybe not. I suppose fame becomes monotonous like everything else. But, I wouldn't want you in the future, to look back and feel that I had stood in your way.

MRS. RITTER. [*Carefully*] No, Fred,—I really don't *know* whether I want to be a great actress or not.

RITTER. But, you are a great actress, dear.

MRS. RITTER. Thank you.

RITTER. [*Indicating the anchor of roses down at the left*] Look at this anchor,—of hope. [*He steps back and picks up the horseshoe.*] And this horseshoe of "SUCCESS." [*He brings it forward and sets it down just to Mrs. Ritter's left. Then he steps across in front of it, takes her hand and slips his right arm around her waist.*] And I think, Paula, it might be a very sensible move, to just let the public *remember* you as a great actress—as they saw you *tonight*—at *your best*.

MRS. RITTER. [*Looking wistfully straight ahead*] Do you think they *will* remember, Fred?

RITTER. [*Inclining his head, with a suggestion of the obsequious*] Yes, I *think* they will. [*Curtain.*]

MRS. RITTER. [*Turning and sinking into his arms*] You're awfully sweet, Fred.

THE END OF THE PLAY